# POWER, INFLUENCE,
## AND AUTHORITY

# POWER, INFLUENCE, AND AUTHORITY

*An Essay in Political Linguistics*

DAVID V. J. BELL
YORK UNIVERSITY

*New York*   OXFORD UNIVERSITY PRESS
*London*   *1975*   *Toronto*

*Matri Patrisque Memoriae*

320.014
B41p
94086
aug 1975

# Acknowledgments

Some books are written; this one seems to have evolved. The first ideas originated in a seminar paper I wrote for Professor Carl Friedrich in 1966. Since then my views have changed considerably in response to "influences" beyond my comprehension. It would be impossible to acknowledge all those who contributed to the evolution of my thinking. I will name only those who have read and commented on this manuscript in its latest versions. These people include Edward Azar, Kaaren C. M. Bell, Karl W. Deutsch, Robert Deutsch, Edgar Dosman, William Eckhardt, Gerry Ginsburg, J. Grant Macdonald, J. D. McFarland, John O'Neill, Graham Reed, Jim Williams, and H. T. Wilson.

In addition, Professor Harold Kaplan prepared an extensive detailed commentary on the penultimate draft of the manuscript: his criticisms and suggestions guided me throughout the final revision.

I should also like to thank Mr. James C. Amon of Oxford University Press, who combines the rare qualities of a superb editor —intelligence, sympathy, patience, and discipline. His talents contributed substantially to the realization of this book. Thanks are due as well to Jo-Anne Degabriele, Leleith Smith, and Anne Lichacz for valuable secretarial assistance; and to Réjean Landry for research help and criticism. A final note of appreciation to the many students, undergraduate and graduate, who have tried to think through and with the concepts presented in this book. They have reconfirmed my belief that good students are the best teachers.

D. V. J. B.

# Contents

**Introduction: New Concepts for Understanding Politics**  3

The Impact of Language on Thought and Perception  5
The Common Sense of Everyday Language  7
Concepts as Paradigms  9
A New Paradigm of Politics  10

**1  Power and Influence**  15

Bases of Influence  26
The Problem of "Costs"  30
"Decoding" Messages  31
Tacit Influence and Tacit Power  33

**2  Authority and Resistance**  35

"Learning" the Credenda of Authority  51
Crises and Breakdowns in Authority  57
Authority and Organization  62
Conclusion  68

**3  Levels of Analysis: The Micro-Macro Problem**  70

Power, Influence, and Authority at the "Micro" Level  71
Power, Influence, and Authority at the Macro Level  81

**Conclusion: Concepts and Action**  91

Studying Politics as Communication  93
A Redefinition of Politics  101
Political Talk and the Presidential Tapes  107

**Appendixes:**  111

A: The Poverty of Political Science Concepts  111
B: A Critique of B. F. Skinner  116

# Preface

This book presents a redefinition of politics in terms of language and communication. Arguing that words and concepts serve as the perceptual lenses through which we "view" the world, the book focuses on three concepts of central importance to the "world of politics"—power, influence, and authority. Each term refers to a linguistic mode of interacting with others to affect their behavior, attitude, or values. Each mode has a peculiar language or style discussed and illustrated by means of paradigm examples and illustrations. But the "real world" of these modes of interaction goes far beyond the simple paradigms: a full inventory of political communications would range from such "power communications" as threats, bribes, and extortions, through "influence communications" involving suggestions or advice, to "authority communications" expressed as commands, orders, or instructions. Any given communication usually constitutes a tactic in an overall political strategy. The book is therefore more than a cognitive reinterpretation of

---

* To argue that everyday interactions are political is not to overlook the fact that politics goes on at many different levels. The distinction between the politics of everyone's household and the politics of the White House turns however on the consequences of political talk at the highest level rather than on the medium through which it occurs. Thanks to the Presidential transcripts, the whole world knows that Presidential talk resembles our own, down to the expletives we do not delete. What the "head of the household" says nevertheless affects very few; the words of the head of the state may have global consequences.

politics, designed to help us see better the political aspects of language and the communications aspects of politics. It concerns as well our own political activities, for we are all political beings in our everyday life.* To the extent that we communicate with students in an effort to "teach" them, or with members of our family to get them to "do us a favor" or with people at work to "talk them into" adopting a new policy, we are engaged in the "politics" of the classroom, family, or office.

To define as "political" the relationships between parents and children, teachers and students, or even friends and acquaintances, forces reconsideration of the ethical problems surrounding linguistic behavior. If what we do and say affects others, then we must view our words and deeds as forms of political action. It has long been customary to debate the ethics of exercising governmental authority. It is imperative that we treat seriously the ethical implications of exercising power and influence as well. Thus the purpose of this book is not merely to show "how to do things with words" efficiently. For "political coaching" one might more appropriately turn to the dozens of manuals on manipulation, from *The Prince* to *How to Win Friends and Influence People*.

Much closer to the normative goals of this book is Lenny Bruce's shocking but effective use of vulgar speech to shatter the comfortable illusions and hypocrisies embedded in middle-class talk about race, sex, and war. (See his autobiography, *How to Talk Dirty and Influence People*.) Political linguistics must never confine itself to the empirical analysis of political interactions in a moral vacuum. George Orwell's satire on "Newspeak" and Herbert Marcuse's critique of "one dimensional" thought help stimulate a critical consciousness of the dangers inherent in the abuse of language. For while language is the medium of politics, it is far from a neutral instrument. Our own words and vocabulary affect us politically. Language is more than a tool for manipulating others. In ways often undetected, it structures our ideas about those with whom we interact. The medium of politics is itself political. The decay and abuse of language represent a deterioration of political life. A political revolution may require a regeneration (or decolonization?) of vocabulary. The reverse may also be true. Hence, the book focuses much attention on Watergate in an effort to diagnose the malady afflicting the American body politic. The political linguistics approach provides a framework for interpreting and evaluating a political world in which supporters of a Presidential reelection campaign tried to "bug" the Democratic National Headquarters so they could "listen in" on their opponents' political talk; and "covert operations" were used against a researcher who had the temerity to publish papers relating secret conversations and memoranda on America's involvement in the Vietnam war; and for the first time in history the American President resigned, after some of his conversations with his aides became a matter of public record.

As we must accustom our ears to the sounds of politics, so we must show sensitivity to the significance of political silence. It is a great mistake to confound silence with agreement, or even with acquiescence. Silence may mask oppression. "Things are quiet" in a police state because no one is permitted to "speak out" —in word or deed—against the state. The politically silent are often the "wretched of the earth." * When they break the silence that has muted their misery, sometimes they speak with actions rather than words, in shrill tones of violence and destruction.

In an ideal political community, on the other hand, people listen to each other's talk, especially their urgent words, rendering

---

* "Silence is the ultimate political tragedy of language. Silence is the special fate of colonial societies, and thus men like Fanon and Freire have been deeply concerned with the crucial relationship between politics and language in the experience of oppression and the struggle for decolonization." John O'Neill, "Language and Decolonization: Fanon and Freire." French translation under the title "Le Langage et La Décolonisation" appears in *Sociologie et Société* VI, 2 Nov. 1974. See also O'Neill's "Violence, Technology and the Body Politic" in Sherman M. Stanage (ed.) *Reason and Violence* (Totowa, N.J.: Littlefield, Adams and Co., 1974). I am grateful to Professor O'Neill for his penetrating comments on an early draft of this Preface.

violence unnecessary as a form of political communication. The humanization of society consists of our learning to talk and listen together. Thus a prime educational task for political linguistics concerns the necessity of understanding how political communication can make political community, both within nation states and among them, possible. The requisite pedagogy has never been systematized, though Paulo Freire offers some valuable beginnings. Everyone, he insists, including the oppressed, must first learn to "speak to their condition":

> Human existence cannot be silent nor can it be nourished by false words, but only by true words, with which men transform the world. To exist, humanly, is to *name* the world, to change it. . . . [Saying true words] is not the privilege of some few men, but the right of every man.*

Perhaps one day the theory and practice of political linguistics will come together in a praxis of political understanding, when the poor and weak will learn to speak and the rich and strong will learn to listen.

*Thornhill, Ontario*                                        D. V. J. B.
*January 12, 1975*

---

* Paulo Freire, *Pedagogy of the Oppressed* (New York: The Seabury Press, 1970), p. 76.

# POWER, INFLUENCE,
## AND AUTHORITY

# Introduction:
# New Concepts for
# Understanding Politics

Pennsylvania Senator Richard Schweiker . . . complained in a radio and television broadcast that Canada's decision to raise the [oil export] tax . . . is "gouging." . . . "[If our Canadian cousins] are going to gouge us . . . I think we ought to look at the auto parts agreement that we favourably have given to their country. . . ."

The Toronto Star, January 16, 1974

A Toronto fireman and a clergyman who dreads heights spent 90 minutes talking a 16-year-old boy out of jumping 326 feet from the top of City Hall yesterday. . . . None of their arguments and promises worked until the fireman persuaded the youth that the minister was half frozen.

The Toronto Star, January 15, 1974

P. ". . . I will not talk to you again until you have something to report to me."
D. "All right, Sir."
P. "But I think it is very important that you have these talks with our good friend Kleindienst."
D. "That will be done."

P.    "Tell him we have to get these things worked out. We
have to work together on this thing."
President Nixon to John Dean, February 28, 1973

International intimidation, a local human interest story, and
Presidential plotting—what do they have in common? What we
"see" in these three examples depends on the conceptual lens
through which we view them. This book offers a set of interrelated concepts—power, influence, and authority—designed to
bring politics into focus.

Before we can understand politics, much less quantify and
measure it, we must conceptualize it. To make any sense of the
question "Who holds the power in this community?" we must
have an explicit and elaborate understanding of what we mean
to include within the concept of power. This point applies just as
forcefully to the well-established political scientist as to the freshman taking the first introductory course, or indeed to the "general
reader." We see the world through concepts. Thus, rather than
empirically analyzing the actual "distribution of power in American society," or "the disintegration of authority in the modern
state," this book investigates how one might conceptualize power,
influence, and authority in order to undertake such studies, or to
improve our everyday understanding of the relationships to which
they refer.[1]

1.  "I apprehend the reality of everyday life as an ordered reality. Its phenomena are prearranged in patterns that seem to be independent of my
apprehension of them and that impose themselves upon the latter. The
reality of everyday life appears already objectified, that is, constituted
by an order of objectives that have been designated *as* objects before
my appearance on the scene. The language used in everyday life con-
tinuously provides me with the necessary objectifications and posits the
order within which these make sense and within which everyday life
has meaning for me." Peter L. Berger and Thomas Luckmann, *The
Social Construction of Reality* (New York: Anchor Books, 1967), pp.
21–22.

THE IMPACT OF LANGUAGE ON THOUGHT
AND PERCEPTION

It is by now a fairly well established hypothesis that concepts shape (if they do not wholly determine) perception. For while our experience involves an endless, continuous flow of "sensations" that literally assault our beings, consciousness of these sensations requires that we group them into segments, using concepts, thereby imposing an order which permits us to form perceptions. Such concept formation occurs in virtually every sphere of our experience.

Comparative study of people in sociocultural settings different from our own yields conclusive confirmation that language shapes perception and thought. Anglophones, for example, are accustomed to think of the color spectrum as being segmented into six or seven main colors, ranging from violet to red. Other cultures segment the spectrum into different groups of shadings. Shona (a language of Rhodesia) identifies four segments of the spectrum, while Bassa (a Liberian tongue) recognizes only two. Similarly, the Eskimos have a vocabulary of approximately twenty distinct words for the stuff that in English we call simply "snow." Studies have shown that the poverty or richness of a conceptual lexicon strongly affects the way in which individuals experience the world. We develop richer and more precise concepts to describe those aspects of the world that seem most important. Linguistic differentiation therefore is associated with proximity (in a social rather than simply a physical sense).[2]

This view, of course, undermines the position that "names" are somehow "God-given." As children we tend to assume that the

2. "I experience everyday life in terms of differing degrees of closeness and remoteness, both spatially and temporally. . . . Typically, my interest in the far zones is less intense and certainly less urgent." *Ibid.*, p. 22. The discussion of cross-cultural "lexical mappings of the color spectrum" appears in Roger Brown, *Social Psychology* (New York: Free Press, 1965), pp. 315–16.

choice of a particular name for a particular thing is inevitable, and conversely that for every name there somewhere exists a concrete, natural thing to which it must refer.[3] A sophisticated leap of understanding is required to achieve the realization that names are quite simply conventional. Though concepts (unless they are neological) have a "history" in the course of which they have taken on meanings that are both denotational and connotational, the original decision to attach a certain meaning to a certain term is arbitrary. A rose by any other name would be called something else.

In this book a systematic distinction is maintained among three types of social interactions, designated by the terms power, influence, and authority. Now in a certain sense the choice of labels for these categories is arbitrary: instead of power, influence, and authority we might have used the labels alpha, beta, and gamma. The three terms chosen do have a conceptual history, however, which favors the meanings attached to them. I am suggesting, therefore, that we segment our understanding of this type of political relationship into at least three, rather than merely one or two conceptual categories.[4] Perhaps this advice should be considered alongside the proposition that the world up close is conceptually more differentiated than the world at a distance as an attempt to get "closer" to politics, to give the world of politics more "texture."

3.  "Language appears to the child as inherent in the nature of things, and he cannot grasp the notion of its conventionality. A thing *is* what it is called, and it could not be called anything else." Berger and Luckmann, *op. cit.,* p. 59.
4.  Most contemporary political scientists formally define power and influence as interchangeable synonyms, and occasionally throw authority into this undifferentiated mass as well. In this respect, the formal language of professional political science analysis is impoverished in comparison even to everyday speech. For a more elaborate discussion see Appendix A.

## THE COMMON SENSE OF EVERYDAY LANGUAGE

If contemporary political science terminology is poverty-stricken, everyday language represents an embarrassment of riches. In contrast to the arid and narrow "scholarly" definition of a term like power, which is then stretched to cover literally a multitude of sins, our day-to-day experience throws up a host of terms which describe in implicit detail a vast range of qualitatively different relationships: manipulation, guidance, counseling, pressure, hypnosis, suggestion, extortion, blackmail, coercion, advising, instructing, commanding, demanding. Similarly, we possess a sophisticated repertoire of concepts which outline appropriate responses to these initiatives: acceptance, agreement, obedience, capitulation, resistance, opposition, and so on. Each of these terms serves a dual function, on the one hand giving an empirical account of the relationship and on the other conveying a normative evaluation of it. This dual function is served almost unconsciously by a kind of interpretive osmosis, inevitably enriched by such nonverbal signals as facial expression and voice intonation.

A great deal of interpersonal communication appears as an attempt to "locate" with words and other signals the qualitative coordinates of a given relationship along a finely textured matrix of interactions. For the student of human interaction, the meticulous detail of everyday language must, however, itself be arranged into clusters or patterns, without treating all varieties as an undifferentiated lump. The choice for this purpose of a trinity of concepts—power, influence, and authority—is not inspired by any religious parallels (although the fascination with trichotomies mysteriously crops up in thinkers as diverse as Plato, Marx, and Freud, thus implying some type of "invisible force"). Instead it represents an effort to "segment" a certain type of interaction into three admittedly arbitrary categories. We are to a distressing extent hampered in this effort by the medium of print. Were this exploration taking place in a face-to-face encounter there would be no need to restrict the focus to a small number of concepts. We could range over the whole matrix of interactions, choosing terms that seemed mutually appropriate, only defining them if we sensed in each other's face or voice a trace of ambiguity or confusion. But print is hard and fast, and mercilessly permanent and inflexible. Everything must be stated precisely and consistently. Delicate shadings (conveyed in speech by gesture, intonation, and formal expression) are hard to capture in writing.[5] My hope is to improve on other conceptual schemes already in print or to raise to a level of consciousness sensitivities that are implicit in our everyday language even while they are absent from our theoretical jargon.

Of our trinity of concepts, perhaps the greatest is power. Certainly, through its links with notions of potency, virility, and masculinity, it appears much sexier than the other two. We speak of being "close to the center of power," but do we ever refer to the "centers of influence"? Of course we discuss "networks of influence"; we sometimes ask people to "use their influence in Washington" (or in Ottawa); we may lament that our children have been "exposed to a bad influence." We note with regret that some parapolitical actors "peddle influence." Politicians deny that they were "influenced" to award contracts to campaign donors. And finally, we refer to "crises" or "breakdowns in authority," we accuse people of "over-stepping their authority," or of "acting without proper authority," we damn an individual by describing him as "authoritarian," we praise him by saying that he is "authoritative," and we insist that leaders "exercise their authority" to steer us through difficult times. Thus our everyday language furnishes us with a rather comprehensive set of linguistic symbols to help us pick our way through the complex maze of political re-

5.  ". . . [W]ritten discourse cannot be 'rescued' by all the processes by which spoken discourse supports itself in order to be understood—intonation, delivery, mimicry, gestures." Paul Ricoeur, "The Model of the Text: Meaningful Action Considered as a Text," *Social Research,* XXXVIII, Autumn 1971, pp. 534–35.

lationships, in order both to recognize the landscape and to react to it in an intelligent and appropriate manner. Our everyday political language is, in short, both cognitive and evaluative.

## CONCEPTS AS PARADIGMS

If a concept serves as a sort of perceptual lens, a cluster of interrelated concepts can provide what amounts to a "world view." Students of political theory have known for a long time that each theorist in effect "paints a picture of politics" derived from his own unique "angle of vision." But this is a picture composed of verbal concepts rather than visual images. Such pictures, moreover, can be compared to the "paradigms" intrinsic to all scientific theories.[6] The Ptolemaic paradigm pictured the earth at the center of the universe.

Whenever a paradigm becomes widely accepted or shared among a group of scientists, we can speak of a process of "normal science" during which puzzles related to the paradigm are "solved," thereby enhancing the scientists' belief that the paradigm is a "valid" picture of "reality." Occasionally, though perhaps inevitably, there arise certain "anomalies" which undermine the validity of the paradigm. Science enters a period of crisis, in which conflict occurs regarding the status of the "old" paradigm and the attractiveness of any "new" contenders. (This conflict can be rather brutal: Galileo was threatened with death unless he "recanted" his challenge to the Ptolemaic paradigm.) But such conflicts are often resolved through the occurrence of what Thomas Kuhn calls a "scientific revolution," in the course of which a single paradigm

6.   For a fascinating discussion of more of these points see Sheldon Wolin, *Politics and Vision* (Boston: Little, Brown, 1960), ch. 1, and "Paradigms and Politics," in Preston King and B. C. Parekh, eds., *Politics and Experience* (Cambridge, at the University Press, 1968). The notion of paradigm is developed by Thomas Kuhn in *The Structure of Scientific Revolutions,* 2nd ed. (Chicago: University of Chicago Press, 1969).

can predominate and scientists once again—or perhaps for the first time—come to share a world view with respect to their particular field of study.

To the extent that power, influence, and authority are concepts of central importance to the study of politics, any effort to redefine them has implications for a political science paradigm. At the very least, the meaning of "politics" itself will be transformed.

A NEW PARADIGM OF POLITICS

Politics is talk. An oversimplification, of course, but one that ultimately lies closer to the truth than definitions like "who gets what, when, how." "Getting" can be an intensely private affair; talk (ordinarily) involves others. Not by accident does the term Parliament stem from the French *parler,* to speak. But politics is more than "a government of talk," because government itself is too restrictive. Much non- or even anti-governmental talk is political nonetheless.

Is all talk political? Perhaps. To the extent that talk *affects* others (and most talk does), it has by definition assumed political overtones. For politics must be concerned in the widest sense with how people affect each other. A suitable reformulation might be, *politics: who talks to whom, when, how.* Of *definite* political significance are the three kinds of talk identified in this book: power talk, influence talk, and authority talk. (What I mean by these terms will soon become clear.)

Talk is, of course, guided by certain rules not only of grammar but also of "social appropriateness." Notice how many different styles of talk we use, how we adjust our vocabulary, our tone of voice, our voice level, and even the content of our conversation to "the situation." Thus we have "pillow talk," "small talk," "cocktail conversation," "shop talk," "sweet talk," and so on. We scold children for "talking back" to their parents. We bristle when someone "talks sharply" to another, perhaps expecting a reply in "fighting words." Governments generate their own linguistic categories, including "strong talk," "election talk," "testimony," "formal statement," "official comment," "diplomatic talk," "negotiation," and, after the Presidential transcripts, "stonewall" (a verb that appears to connote "refusal to talk"). People often demand "a say" in their government. Authoritarian regimes often react severely to "dissidents" who "speak out" against the Establishment. The expulsion of Alexander Solzhenitsyn from the Soviet Union provides a striking case in point.

As students of politics, we should appreciate that talk, in the wider sense connoted by "communication," can take many forms ranging from written messages to signals and gestures. Clubbing someone over the head is one rather primitive way of "signaling" a message; dropping an atomic bomb is another. Putting a full-page advertisement in a national magazine, though generally a more sophisticated signaling technique, may be less effective. Communication, in short, is a widely diverse social phenomenon that often produces quite unpredictable results.

The other side of the communications coin is listening: who listens to whom, and what difference does it make? Obviously all talk is not "created equal." Certain words carry greater "weight" than others, especially when they are spoken or written by particular individuals. Virtually everything President Nixon and his advisers "said" in the various Oval Office meetings has significance for the interpretation of their involvement in the Watergate cover-up, to the point where individuals charged with the responsibility of assigning guilt and blame insisted on "hearing" the tapes rather than merely reading an edited transcript. The words of a President are very "weighty" indeed.

Furthermore, talk can exist on many levels of "meaning," from the intention of the speaker to the interpretation of the listener. Indeed, it is important to recognize at least three such levels, including the meaning intended by the author of a communication, the meaning ascribed to the communication by an observer, and the meaning interpreted by the receiver who "decodes" the communication. Seldom are these three levels of meaning perfectly congruent. Meaning is to talk what the submerged nine-tenths of an iceberg is to the visible tip. Meaning entails the vast stock of "knowledge" we carry around "in our heads," which affects the way we interpret verbal and nonverbal communication.

But allowing for these imperfections and elaborations, we can use as an organizing assumption or point of departure the axiom that politics is talk. The task of political science, therefore, is to study talk. What do people say, and who listens? What happens next? (One is reminded of Eric Berne's posthumous publication, *What Do You Say After You Say Hello?*)

*Power, Influence, and Authority* explores ways in which we can usefully classify and analyze political talk. It redefines these traditional concepts in terms of linguistic categories, suggesting that each consists of a special, distinct form of communication. Through many techniques and devices, I attempt to "influence" the reader to a linguistic point of view. While old hat in some fields, a linguistic approach represents a rather new departure for the study of politics. Some scholars would probably scoff at such overemphasis on "words" (*verba*) instead of "deeds" (*facta*). Seen properly, however, the *verba-facta* distinction poses a false dichotomy: most political deeds turn out to be built of and around words. (The proverb "Actions *speak louder* than words" nevertheless acknowledges that both are forms of communication.) Think about a "declaration of war," a "negotiated peace settlement" or an "executive order." And even "deeds" that are manifestly nonverbal (like many "acts of war") ultimately must be interpreted within a linguistic framework. We think with words and we see the world through them.

If words in general are very important, the terms power, influence, and authority hold special significance for students of politics (including laymen as well as professionals). The terms are far from self-explanatory or self-evident. The way we define them therefore conditions our entire outlook on politics and government.

Traditional definitions of government and the state proceed swiftly to the "blood and guts" of politics, defining the state in terms of its "monopoly on the legitimate use of coercion and violence." However romantic and exciting, this definition lies far removed from the realities of everyday political life. Not only is overt governmental violence almost nonexistent for most citizens, but even its infrequent use violates the majority's notion of legitimacy and usually indicates a breakdown in authority. In advanced industrial societies, the only organization that uses violence regularly as part of its everyday politics is the Mafia. The state rules through words, not guns. To counter that the words of the state are unique because they are "backed" by violence is misleading on two grounds: in the first place, not all governmental decrees are so backed; in the second place, many nongovernmental words *are* so backed; moreover, the focus on violence-as-backing detracts attention from the words themselves.

Nor can a modern state achieve a comfortable monopoly over the use of social communication. Consequently the authority of the state is uncertain and unabsolute, constantly threatened by alternative organized and unorganized word users.[7] The ratio of words to bullets in any modern government must surely be a million to one. More importantly, the words are used every day, while the bullets may never be fired (because no one has "told" the soldiers that they can or should shoot).

On the rare occasions when violence silences talk, we immediately recognize with Clausewitz that violence is merely the continuation of "power communication" by other, more traumatic,

---

7.  In a public lecture at York University, Marshall McLuhan pointed out that while the Gutenberg Revolution made everyone a "reader," the Xerox Revolution had made everyone a "publisher." The Pentagon Papers represent only one of countless instances of "leaks" of secret government documents made possible in part of advances in photocopying techniques, which may ultimately serve to countervail the repressive impact of insidious electronic surveillance technology.

means: We try to figure out how we should "interpret" the violence. Those who use political violence often do so out of the frustration that arises when other forms of communication repeatedly fail. Several Palestinians (interviewed by NBC) explained their resort to terrorism by insisting that for years "nobody would listen" to their outcry so now they were merely "speaking louder" with bullets and bombs. The principal aim of terrorism is not to destroy but "to be heard," and to convince others of the seriousness of a cause. Unlike personal violence, which is usually purely destructive, political violence serves at least a dual purpose: while it is destructive vis-à-vis its immediate victims, it serves as a form of communication vis-à-vis various target groups such as "world opinion." A political killing is like a message in code.

# Power and Influence

Power, influence, and authority—in everyday speech, their meanings overlap; the terms are sometimes used interchangeably. But at other times they conjure quite different images. There are at least some circumstances in which we would not substitute one of these three terms for the other. To describe a man as powerful is not the same as calling him "influential"; and neither term captures the connotations of the adjective "authoritative." We would hardly find appropriate a book entitled *How to Win Friends and Overpower People.* Nor would we speak of an armed robber "exerting his authority" to obtain cash from a teller.

Presumably, therefore, power, influence, and authority are not perfectly congruent synonyms. Yet even sophisticated students of politics have usually failed to distinguish them. Hannah Arendt must be credited with a sharp understanding of the costs of such linguistic insensitivity:

> It is, I think, a rather sad reflection on the present state of political science that our terminology does not distinguish among such key words as "power," "strength," "force," "authority," and finally "violence" . . . To use them as synonyms not

only indicates a certain deafness to linguistic meanings, which
would be serious enough, but it has also resulted in a kind of
blindness to the realities they correspond to.[1]

But with what methodology are we to arrive at the "correct" means
for distinguishing among these terms? Do we turn to etymology in
the hope of finding the key? Or do we instead decree, as it were,
that the terms mean exactly what we wish? Although I firmly
believe that the failure to draw important distinctions has led to
analytic confusion and meaningless debate, this position poses a
logical and linguistic dilemma: to argue that the words must be
distinguished because they intrinsically mean different things is to
adopt an essentialist position that is indefensible; while to argue
that the words can mean whatever we want them to mean is to
adopt the equally indefensible posture of Humpty Dumpty, who
insisted that he could "make" words mean whatever he wanted
because he was their "master." (He admitted, however, to "pay-
ing" them extra "when he made them do a lot of work.")

My position is made more difficult by the fact that even while
agreeing wholeheartedly with Hannah Arendt's plea for distinctions, I find myself unable to accept her own definitions of the
terms. Obviously there is a great deal of "private vision" in the
picture of politics each writer draws.

To identify differing patterns of social/political relationships
without resorting to neologisms, an investigation of these concepts
must proceed along a path that runs between inductive "discovery"
of "intrinsic" meanings and the deductive pronouncement of arbitrary definitions. Throughout, I place considerable emphasis on
the "common sense" usages of the terms while recognizing that at
times our everyday language is inconsistent and self-contradictory.
The goal of this investigation is to find concepts that illuminate
politics, or—more accurately—bring it into focus. We view the
political world through a series of conceptual lenses which in
turn allow us to see certain features. Clear conceptual vision pre-

1.  Hannah Arendt, *On Violence* (New York: Harcourt, Brace, 1970),
    p. 43.

determines the quality of analysis—both empirical and normative
—that may follow.

Power, influence, and authority refer to certain forms of human relations, that is, these phenomena exist only in a plural
setting where two or more people interact with each other.[2] That
these phenomena are *relational* seems quite obvious, and yet it is
often forgotten. Perhaps because our language is virtually choked
with a plethora of nouns rather than verbs, we tend to assume that
power especially is a concrete thing that an individual can somehow "possess" like a fast car or a lot of money. But this usage is
quite misleading, for, in the words of Eric Hoffer, "Power does
not come in cans." To talk about power as a possession is therefore elliptical. What is really meant by the assertion "A possesses
power" is that A "possesses" the *potential* for exercising power
effectively.[3] In this discussion we will carefully distinguish between "potential power" and power. The former, of course, implies the existence of certain power *resources* that may be used in
the attempt to exercise power.

2.  Note that the term *relation* can imply a repetitive, almost institutional
    quality of interaction and not merely a single disconnected act. "Power
    *relations* are built of repetitive, durable patterns of action, but micro-
    sociological taxonomic schemes, when stretched beyond their useful
    limits, tend to dissolve relation into individual acts." E. V. Walter,
    "Power and Violence," *American Political Science Review* LVIII, 2,
    June 1964, p. 352.
3.  "Unfortunately, power lacks a verb form, which in part accounts for
    the frequent tendency to see it as a mysterious property or agency
    resident in the person or group to whom it is attributed. The use of
    such terms as 'influence' and 'control,' which are both nouns and
    verbs, as virtual synonyms for power, represents an effort (not neces-
    sarily fully conscious) to avoid the suggestion that power is a property
    rather than a relation." Dennis H. Wrong, "Some Problems in De-
    fining Social Power," in Hans P. Dreitzel, ed., *Recent Sociology* No. I
    (London: Macmillan, 1969). Cf. also Wrong's use (following Gil-
    bert Ryle) of the notion of "dispositional" as contrasted with "epi-
    sodic" words to distinguish potential power from the exercise of
    power.

Similarly, authority is not something that can literally be held, although the symbols of authority are often quite tangible. Authority is a relationship between a superordinate and one or more subordinates which, when "activated" by communication, leads to compliance with "orders" or "commands" issued from above. Finally, someone who "has a lot of influence" is an individual who either has influenced many people in the past or is likely to be able to do so in the future. His analogue in the economy is the person who "has a lot of credit," which is not equivalent to "having a lot of money."

Following our axiom that "politics is talk," we wish to discover in general what kind of communication among actors can affect their action, and then proceed to a further subdivision of this kind of communication into three categories. Let us narrow our initial interest to communications expressed in words rather than other nonverbal signals such as gestures.

At first glance our task seems more akin to linguistics than political science, for we are concerned with identifying verbal communication that can be understood or comprehended. Suppose that the structure of a shared language is understood by two actors A and B. Obviously, the rules of grammar and syntax for their language limit the sentences A and B can construct and understand. But within these constraints, what types of sentences are likely to affect their action?

The problem is that almost anything said by A can under certain circumstances affect B's action, perhaps substantially. For example, B may be so upset over something that if A even says "Boo," B will burst into tears. Ordinarily "boo" seems quite innocuous. It is probably impossible to construct a theory that will allow us to predict in advance whether a given sentence or expression will affect a given actor in a particular way.

The English philosopher of language J. L. Austin has elaborated some concepts that illuminate this discussion. In attempting to investigate the "uses" of language, Austin distinguishes among a) the mere act of speech as a proper use of words (locution); b) the uttering of a sentence as an act-in-itself, e.g., saying the marriage vows before a minister (illocution); and c) the "successful" use of words to bring about an action on someone else's part, e.g., issuing an order which is then obeyed (perlocution). But Austin further distinguishes words with a perlocutionary *object* from those which merely give rise to a perlocutionary *sequel*. In the first instance the effect is *intended,* whereas in the second instance it is not. And while one may fairly easily identify in advance statements that have (intended) perlocutionary objects, it is virtually impossible to predict which statements will have (unintended) perlocutionary *sequels*. "For clearly *any,* or almost any, perlocutionary act is liable to be brought off, in sufficiently special circumstances, by the issuing, with or without calculation, of any utterance whatsoever. . . ." [4]

More progress can be made if we first pick out certain types of verbal communication that express identifiable relationships in the form of either threats or promises. While in everyday encounters a threat may be conveyed by a mere gesture or even a raised eyebrow, verbal threats display remarkable uniformity of logical structure. They take the form of hypothetical or contingent statements[5] expressed in the "first person":

4.  Cf. also the following: "A judge should be able to decide, by hearing what was said, what locutionary and illocutionary acts were performed, but not what perlocutionary acts were achieved." I shall say more about Austin's analysis below. J. L. Austin, *How to Do Things with Words* (Cambridge, Mass.: Harvard University Press, 1962), pp. 109, 121.

5.  It is also possible, as John Searle (*Speech Acts,* Cambridge: Cambridge University Press, 1969, pp. 55–56) has pointed out, to make "categorical" threats and promises. These would be expressed in the simple declaration "I will do X." But categorical threats are usually made in some sort of context which implies a contingency. A "normal" person simply does not go around uttering (or muttering) threats "for no reason." This fact was tragically illustrated in the case of the resident of Hamilton, Ontario, who earned the nickname "Me Shoot" because he frequently uttered this categorical threat in the course of arguments. One day during a dispute about a fence he shot to death three neighbors.

If you do X, *I* will do Y.

This simple paradigm can be "filled in" with appropriate symbols or words to represent any given "threat-communication." For example, "If you say that again, I'll break your neck." Here the form of the threat follows exactly the form of the paradigm. But the basic structure remains the same even if we change the "sign" of X from positive to negative: "If you do *not* give me your money, I'll blow your brains out." Of course a would-be holdup man might very well use a different construction from the paradigm. He might say "Your money or your life." Or he might simply brandish a gun and say, "Give me your money." But implicit within the context of this situation is a threat which, were it not for the ellipsis of action and gesture, would take the basic form of the paradigm.

Thus in a threat-communication, the performance of action Y by the "threatener" is made contingent on the performance (or nonperformance) of action X by the recipient of the threat. In other words, action Y is the penalty you must pay if you refuse to comply with my demand that you do X. But what is it about action Y that makes it a penalty for you? Clearly, action Y must involve some loss or pain or suffering on your part; you must stand to lose something by my performing action Y, or else my threat would be "empty." We can describe Y, therefore, as a *sanction* which I will apply if you fail to comply. And since we are here concerned with threats, action Y can be further described as a *negative* sanction. It would make little sense whatever if as a "penalty" for noncompliance I "threatened" you with a "sanction" that consisted in some action you found immensely enjoyable. Indeed, this is one reason why it is difficult to use threats effectively against a masochist. Presumably his desire for pain and punishment transmutes "negative sanctions" into a source of pleasure. In the end, however, the plight of the masochist is pathetic. Like Oscar on Sesame Street, the masochist finds himself in an infinite regress of contradictory sentiments. He is only happy when he is sad, so being sad makes him happy. But this of course makes him sad which in turn makes him happy . . . , etc.

The agonizing ambivalence of the masochist under threat should not obscure the fact that the "nonsense" of a pleasurable threat is semantical nonsense only. The world is full of pleasurable threats, except that we call them by a different name—promises. From this perspective, a promise is simply a positive threat, or rather a first-person hypothetical in which the "Y" is a positive sanction.[6] "If you go to bed with me, I'll give you fifty dollars." Or, as the popular kiddies' song has it, "If you show me yours, I'll show you mine." Here again, X may be either negative or positive: "If you *don't* tell mother, I'll let you play with my truck." In short, threats and promises share an identical syntactical structure illustrated in the paradigm,

If you do X, I will do Y,

where X and Y may each be either positive or negative.

It is to communications which involve either threats or promises that I wish to attach the name *power*. Notice that this usage makes no presuppositions about the likely effectiveness of a power communication. I am decidedly not assuming that power will result in compliance, or conversely that compliance must occur before power can be said to exist. Rather the concept refers to a certain relationship, embodied in a communication, by which A presents B with an "offer" to which is attached a contingency in the form of a reward (promise) or a penalty (threat).

It may at first appear curious (and perhaps misleading) to classify threats and promises together under the category of

6. Cf. Searle, *ibid.*, p. 58: "One crucial distinction between promises on the one hand and threats on the other is that a promise is a pledge to do something for you not to you; but a threat is a pledge to do something to you not for you." See also his list of nine "conditions" for promising.

power.[7] Behavioral psychologists have carried out numerous studies to show the differential effectiveness of what they call positive versus negative "reinforcements." A common finding is that positive reinforcement is less likely to inspire hostility or resentment and therefore functions more effectively, especially in learning situations. Regardless of specific findings, the point is that experimental psychology has uncovered important reasons for distinguishing between negative and positive types of reinforcement. I have no intention of trying to refute such findings, nor do I propose that we overlook the differences between threat-power and promise-power. The rationale for the decision to classify them both under the concept of power will become apparent when we investigate the meaning I have given to the notion of influence.

However much threats and promises differ with respect to the reactions they may engender, the degree to which they represent "coercion," etc., they nevertheless share a number of crucial characteristics. Structurally, as I have already shown, they are identical (i.e., both can be reduced to the paradigm, "If you do X, I will do Y"). But they are alike in another way as well. If we imagine an individual as occupying (at a given point in time) a certain

---

7.  Other writers, most notably Talcott Parsons, have used the distinction between positive and negative sanctions itself as the basis for distinguishing influence from power. Thus, for Parsons, power involves "mobilizing the performance binding obligations [of others], with the conditional implication of the imposition of negative sanctions." Influence, by contrast, operates through the use of what Parsons calls positive "intentional" sanctions. The term *intentional* is introduced to distinguish "influence" from "money." The latter also operates through the use of positive sanctions, which are "situational." Thus the two types of positive sanctions permit Parsons to distinguish between "inducement" and "persuasion." Ultimately there are several similarities between Parsons' concept of influence and my own. I do feel, however, that the term "sanction" is inappropriate to his discussion of persuasion, and should be reserved for what he calls inducement. Furthermore, I would include "negative intentional" relations under influence, and "positive situational" relations under power. See Talcott Parsons, "On the Concept of Influence," *Public Opinion Quarterly*, XXVII, 1 Spring, 1963 p. 44.

"position" along various continua with respect to several different values—wealth, security, knowledge, personal health, etc.,—then power takes the form of a declared intent to "shift" the individual's value position either in the direction of *more* enjoyment of the value (promise) or of *less* (threat). The promise is "kept" only if compliance is forthcoming, whereas the threat is "carried through" if compliance is *not*. But the outcome is identical: the individual in either case is "better off" (i.e., more favorably positioned along the value continua) if he complies than if he does not. In the first instance, he actually moves "ahead" whereas in the second instance he avoids being moved "back." Furthermore, even a positive sanction can be manipulated negatively if our "supplier" threatens to "cut us off." Absence of reward is in many instances equivalent to punishment.

The notion I am struggling so awkwardly to express in academic prose was made unforgettably vivid in the novel/movie *The Godfather*. Michael is explaining to his girlfriend how his father, Don Corleone, managed to secure the release of the singer Johnnie Fontaine from an unfair but legally binding contract. Don Corleone went to the bandleader who held the contract and offered him $10,000 if he would release Fontaine. The bandleader refused.

"The next day my father went back to see the bandleader. He went in with a certified check for $1,000 and came out with a signed release."

"How did he do that?" asked Kay.

"He made the bandleader an offer he couldn't refuse."

"You mean more money?"

"Not exactly. This time my father took Luco Brasi with him when he went to see the bandleader. Luco held a gun to the bandleader's head and my father told him 'Either your signature or your brains are going to be on this contract.' . . ."

In view of the popularity (or notoriety) of *The Godfather*, no future reference to "making an offer that can't be refused" will escape ambiguity: does it refer to an unusually large positive sanction or to a painfully compelling negative sanction?

To this point, we have merely succeeded in identifying power communications by referring to their structure and intent. In effect we have skated around such important issues (which will be taken up later) as how an individual gets into a position to issue a power communication, under what conditions such communications are "credible," and whether power will indeed result in compliance. Similarly, we have failed to examine the alternative responses to power communications.[8] Nor have we said anything to illuminate the phenomenon of power in large-scale, complex social units. Indeed, most of our remarks have assumed a "dyadic" (i.e., one-to-one) relationship between only two actors, A and B. But the analysis so far has at least set the stage for an elaboration of the concept of *influence,* which we define as a communication intended to affect the action of B in the absence of sanctions (i.e., threats or promises).

How then does influence work? Let us examine the syntactical structure of an influence communication, even though this exercise is only a partially satisfactory description of influence (which ultimately serves as a kind of residual category for nonpower, nonauthority relations). The problem we face is this: can a relationship between two actors avoid threats and promises and yet be "important"? To put it differently, can we construct a sentence that does not take the form of a threat or promise but is nevertheless capable of affecting someone else's action?

Surprisingly, the basic power paradigm requires very little modification to provide at least one "solution" to this problem, thereby "proving" the possibility of influence. To transform the

8.  In most instances, the uttering of a promise or threat occurs as a "move" in a social "interchange." It will usually be followed by at least one more move (i.e., response by B) and possibly further moves by both actors. For the concepts of interchange and move, see Erving Goffman, *Interaction Ritual* (New York: Anchor Books, 1967), p. 20.

threat/promise expressed in first-person contingent statements into a sanction-free influence statement, we need only introduce the second-person construction:

> If you do X, *you* will do (feel, experience, etc.) Y
> (second-person contingent statement).

The effect of this minute change is profound. Contrast the power communication, "If you marry that girl, I'll cut you out of my will" with the far subtler influence communication, "If you marry that girl, you'll be miserable for the rest of your life!" In place of a threat or promise, influence involves a kind of *prediction* in the form of advice, encouragement, warning, and so on. "Advice is cheap," cynics may counter. Yes, but advisers are often very highly paid. Figure that one out.

The assertion that influence is sanction-free does not necessarily contradict the assumption that human behavior is shaped or generated by contingencies of reinforcement.[9] The "prediction" that "you will be miserable" indeed forecasts a very undesirable contingency attendant to your marrying "that girl." The difference is that this contingency, unlike the act of cutting you out of "my will," is *not* being manipulated by "me." To forewarn of a "threatening situation" is not the same as to make a threat. We would not speak of the weatherman as a "powerful" person, and yet the information he provides often has a considerable "influence" on the plans of millions of people.

Viewed from this perspective, the "influence" of religious leaders can be assimilated to a new version of the influence paradigm. The priest serves in effect as an adviser, predicting a whole range of contingencies (including "fire and brimstone," "everlasting damnation," eternal salvation, etc.) which will be dispensed by God either in this life or the life to come. Thus the new influence paradigm is,

9. For an extended critique of B. F. Skinner's theory of contingent reinforcement, see Appendix B.

If you do X, He (God) will do Y
(third-person contingent statement).

By now it should be clear that while power rests on the ability to manipulate positive or negative sanctions, influence does not. In either the second-person or the third-person contingent statements which we have proposed as paradigms of influence, the influencer, rather than manipulating the contingencies of reinforcement, is attempting to manipulate *perceptions* of those contingencies. He says, in effect, "If you do X, Y will happen," where Y is beyond his control.

### BASES OF INFLUENCE

Successful use of power presupposes control (or apparent control) over some *resource* that might serve as a sanction or "contingency of reinforcement." By contrast, successful influence may be said to rest on a variety of *bases* which permit the influencer to change people's perceptions of contingencies or situations controlled by others.

One such basis for influence is prestige. Other things being equal, an actor who has high prestige is influential by virtue of the deference or priority he enjoys in, for example, a communications network, where his messages will be given priority over those of less prestigious actors. This priority can take many forms: it may mean his messages will be transmitted first; or it may mean they are believed first, etc.[10]

Analytically, prestige may be regarded as either positional or personal; that is, prestige may be accorded a position regardless of who occupies the position, or it may be accorded a person en-

10. Some of the psychological mechanisms underlying "prestige influence" are cogently discussed by Roger Brown in his chapter "The Principle of Consistency in Attitude Changes," in *Social Psychology, op. cit.*

tirely apart from whatever position he may happen to occupy
real life, an actor's prestige is a mixture of the prestige of his
sition and his own personal prestige. The ratio of positional to
personal prestige differs for each "role." The role of rich man has
a high ratio of nonpersonal to personal prestige. The role of
charismatic leader has a low ratio. The role of intellectual is somewhere in between—in the academic community, the words of even
the brightest freshman usually carry less prestige, and hence less
influence, than even the most tiresome platitudes of the Distinguished University Professor. Furthermore, prestige may be specific or diffuse. In traditional society, the prestige of the witch
doctor is generalized to his pronouncements on almost any subject
whatever. In modern society, at least theoretically, the doctor's
prestige is usually limited to pronouncements in his field specialty.
Academics are especially jealous of the need to restrict prestige to
areas of specialization. "Professor X may be an expert on physics,
but he knows nothing whatsoever about politics." But even in
advanced industrial societies like the United States prestige in one
field frequently "spills over" into another: witness Dr. Spock's influence as an antiwar leader. When we analyze influence, the degree to which prestige is specific, like the ratio of personal to nonpersonal prestige, is a matter of empirical investigation. But such
investigation would not simply involve compiling certain "objective" data about roles in society. For prestige is manifestly subjective: to find out how much prestige A has one must find out
how *other* actors in the relevant community perceive his role.
Because of this subjective facet, there is considerable variation in
the effectiveness of influence based on prestige. We cannot be sure
that B and C will have identical perceptions of A's prestige, thus
we cannot assume that they will both give equal priority to his
messages.

Beyond the prestige of the person and the prestige of his position, one must also consider the prestige of the messages themselves. Much influence (some forms of advertising, for example)
is divorced from specific persons or positions. In such cases, the

exercise of influence relies on choosing symbols and words that
will create a favorable impression on the prospective respondent.
Underlying all the gimmickry, the message contained in most advertising corresponds to the influence communication, "If you
want to get rich (appear sexy, have a good time, etc.), you should
use our product (service, etc.)."

A third basis of influence may be a debt or obligation on
which the influencer can "collect." Often favors are dispensed
(supposedly without condition) precisely to evoke feelings of in-
debtedness which can later be converted into reciprocal action.
Because the favor (which may take the form of a "gift" of goods,
money, or service) is not stipulated as a sanction, we do not classify this type of relation under the "power" category. In addition
to being uncertain as far as effectiveness is concerned, "debt influence" is almost always an exhaustible resource. Unless the original gift was very large indeed, or unless the favor is conducted
in an ongoing manner, there are limits on the number of times A
may successfully convert B's sense of obligation into compliance.
It has been suggested, for example, that Lyndon Johnson was able
to call upon numerous debts and obligations, owing him from the
time he was a Senator, to help obtain passage of the Civil Rights
Bill in 1964; but after that time, his influence in the Senate waned
because he had exhausted this considerable resource. Richard
Nixon's successful attainment of the Republican nomination in
1968 was due in large part to the "debt influence" he amassed by
helping other Republican candidates in the 1964 and 1966 cam-
paigns, after he had supposedly withdrawn permanently from active politics. The kind of "message" one might use to "activate"
debt influence could go something like this: "Remember all the
nice things I did for you last year? Well, *if you appreciated them,
you would help me now*."

In every Western polity, "debt influence" is widespread, especially in the context of election campaign contributions. It raises
major ethical and moral issues regarding the limits beyond which
this kind of influence will be considered illegitimate or corrupt. A

supposedly unconditional gift of several hundred thousand dollars to the campaign coffers of a political party is probably not without its benefits after the election has been won.

Conversely, it was learned after the 1972 United States Presidential election that a large number of corporations gave "voluntary" donations to Richard Nixon's campaign that were not so voluntary. These corporations were simply advised that if they knew what was good for them, they would see the wisdom of substantially helping the Committee to Re-Elect the President (CREEP) get its job done. It is not clear who in particular played the role of Luco Brasi in this job of "persuasion," but the ultimate result included a number of indictments for "influence peddling" and some fascinating disclosures about campaign financing. Full disclosure regulations and imposed ceilings on contributions from a single source are measures designed on the one hand to minimize the accumulation of excessive "debt influence" by groups who finance aspiring political leaders, and on the other hand to eliminate the kind of blackmail practiced by CREEP.

While this entire discussion begins to illustrate the difficulty of distinguishing influence from power in several situations, the "ongoing favor" phenomenon presents an extreme case of the problem. When one actor regularly supplies (however "unconditionally") goods or services to another actor who is unable to reciprocate in turn, a situation of dependence obtains, and this may serve as the basis for a power relationship. Indeed, the apparently noncontingent positive rewards can effectively be transformed into negative sanctions since "regular rewards create expectations that redefine the baseline in terms of which positive sanctions are distinguished from negative ones." [11] The consumers of this ongoing favor are "potentially subject" not simply to influence but to power communications as well, unless they can develop strategies for escaping from such dependence (e.g., finding an alternative "supplier," finding a good or service to sell or barter in return,

11.  Peter Blau, *Exchange and Power in Social Life* (New York: Wiley, 1964), p. 117.

learning to do without, etc.). Perhaps the prima facie test of the structure and content of the communication is less illuminating than its "hidden meaning." When a benefactor requests a favor, he can always imply the possibility of sanctions, if only through tone of voice or similar subtlety. (See the discussion below of "decoding" messages.) The demarcation between influence and power is composed of a wide band of "in between" cases, difficult to categorize in one way or the other.

## THE PROBLEM OF "COSTS"

Whereas power is relatively "costly," requiring imposition of a positive or negative sanction, influence appears relatively costless since no sanction is involved. But appearances can deceive: the question of costs involves rather complex considerations. Let's take "threat power." Strictly speaking, a threat that is effective will not require imposition of a sanction. If in response to my threat, you agree not to marry the girl, I will not *have* to cut you out of my will. Nevertheless, to be able to make a serious threat usually requires maintenance of a "threat capability" which may be almost as costly whether it is used or not (e.g., nuclear weapons). In general, the resources for power and influence differ considerably as to the effects of "spending" these resources. As for "promise power," compliance puts the ball back in the power-wielder's court. He must come through with the reward promised as his part of the bargain. Thus promise power rests on control of certain resources that can be used to reward people for compliance with our wishes. The most common and most universally applicable resource of this type is of course money. But virtually any other positively valued commodity—from drugs to sex—can be used as the basis of a "promise power" relationship, provided that the commodity is in relatively scarce supply. To control the behavior of someone facing suffocation in an airtight container, air itself would serve as a highly effective power resource. Given the trends toward air pollution in advanced industrial societies, the promise of fresh air could conceivably generate power over entire populations.

Besides the "direct costs" in terms of the resources underlying power relations, the "exercise" of power (i.e., issuance of a power communication) involves a number of "indirect costs." First there is the "opportunity cost": time and attention devoted to the power relationship could conceivably be "spent" elsewhere, so that an opportunity for alternative activity has been lost. Second, certain "psychic costs" may attend the interaction. The use of power causes many people to feel uncomfortable and may inspire considerable hostility in the "victim." (The sense of exhilaration experienced by some can, however, convert this factor into a positive psychic benefit. We are all acquainted with individuals who like to "take a power trip" and "throw their weight around.") Third, the outcome of the power interaction may affect the power-wielder's *reputation* as a political actor (again the effect may be either beneficial or costly with respect to future interactions). Clearly all three indirect costs inherent in power relations apply to influence relations as well. Thus influence is only less costly with respect to the direct costs involved.[12] Moreover, both relationships carry certain "communication costs." It may be difficult to "locate" the person against whom our power or influence attempt is directed. Phrasing and transmitting the message itself often requires considerable time and effort. Advertising agencies pay copy writers handsome salaries to prepare influential messages.

## "DECODING" MESSAGES

Up to this point we have focused on the initiator or sender of a verbal power or influence message. We have considered the ways in which the message could be phrased, and the costs involved

12. For a sophisticated treatment of this general topic, see David H. Baldwin, "The Costs of Power," *Journal of Conflict Resolution* XV, June 1971. Baldwin points out that the notion of opportunity cost should not be overly restricted: from a certain perspective, all costs are opportunity costs.

in sending it. But what happens at the other end of the communications network? How is the message "received"? In effect we are shifting our attention to the "decoding" phase of a communication process as illustrated in the following diagram:[13]

| Sender | (Encoding  Message  (Decoding | Receiver |
|---|---|---|
| | Process) ⟶ Process) | |

Not all communications are verbal: nor do all verbal communications "mean what they say." Often "hidden messages" lurk behind or within apparently innocuous communications. A stern "good day" may mean that the boss is enraged; a seductive "Well, hello there" may be an invitation to good times. Understanding the hidden meaning in conversation (called by some "meta-talk") requires that we constantly "decode" messages, verbal and nonverbal, to figure out what they "really mean" and how we should respond to them.

Usually the decoding process is tacit and invisible, but it takes place nonetheless "in our heads." In order to classify decoded messages in terms of the concepts of power, influence, and authority, we have merely to invert appropriately our earlier paradigm statements.

A decoded *influence* communication takes the following form: "If I do X, I will experience Y." A decoded power communication takes the form: "If I do X, you will do Y." Despite any apparent ambiguity conjured by these two different paradigms, the distinction is quite clear: in a decoded power communication, we reckon that the author of the message is directly responsible for Y; in a decoded influence communication, someone or something *other than the author* will bring about Y. A decoded "pure" authority message carries with it no contingencies. It would simply take the form "I have been told to do X."

13.  Adapted from Thomas Gordon, *P.E.T. Parent Effectiveness Training* (New York: Peter H. Wyden), 1970. Paulo Freire presents a fascinating discussion of "decoding" as a technique of "co-investigation" designed to "deepen the critical awareness" of "the oppressed." See his *Pedagogy of the Oppressed* (New York: The Seabury Press, 1970), pp. 95–118.

Do people ever "decode" messages incorrectly? Of course they do. Often this is precisely what has happened when we say that a "breakdown of communications" has occurred. "When I told him that 'there would be hell to pay' I only *meant* to give him some advice [influence] but he *thought* I was threatening him [power]. We simply *cannot* communicate with each other."

In addition to the cognitive aspect of a message signified by our power and influence paradigms, most political messages carry concealed *evaluative* meaning. The receiver uncovers this meaning in the course of decoding the message. "He's threatening to cut me out of his will. Who does he think I am, some kind of child? Nobody talks to me like that. Besides, if he really cared for me, he'd put my feelings above his inflated pride. Some father!" As a determinant of the response a given message will inspire, the "hidden meaning" cannot be overemphasized. Yet knowledge of hidden meanings presupposes that we have some insight into the feelings and beliefs of the receiver. Not all people will decode a message identically. Thus the study of power, influence, and authority requires that we engage in creative mind-reading (or what a few sociologists call "in-dwelling" and others "subjective interpretation") in order to understand the reactions that are occurring "inside the heads" of the people concerned.

## TACIT INFLUENCE AND TACIT POWER

Occasionally we find that people decode messages that have never been sent! Indeed, there is a whole range of tacit influence (and indeed tacit power) that falls into the category of "anticipated reactions." [14] An actor tacitly subjects himself to influence or power by *asking himself* questions about the likely outcome of his

14. The "rule of anticipated reactions" was "discovered" by Carl J. Friedrich in 1937 (*Constitutional Government and Politics*, pp. 16–18). A discussion of the rule appears in his *Man and His Government* (New York: McGraw-Hill, 1963), ch. 11. Despite its obvious importance, very little has been done by others to develop the implications of the concept beyond merely citing the rule.

actions. When the self-questioning takes the form of an inverted first person hypothetical, we can speak of tacit power. Thus,

If I do X, will you do Y?

But if the question takes the form of an inverted second- or third-person hypothetical, it represents an example of tacit influence. Erving Goffman splendidly illustrates the point:

> The socialized interactant comes to handle spoken interaction as he would any other kind, as something that must be pursued with ritual care. By automatically appealing to face, he knows how to conduct himself in regard to talk. By repeatedly and automatically asking himself the question, "if I do or do not act in this way, will I or *others* lose face?" he decides at each moment consciously or unconsciously, how to behave.[15]

To the extent that we have learned to be "sociable" animals, we continually anticipate others' reactions to our own behavior. In a sense, sociability implies precisely this consciousness of the social context within which we live. "Inappropriate" behavior stems from either a failure to engage in anticipatory calculation, a miscalculation of probable reaction, or the willfully perverse determination to act in a certain way "regardless of what others say." Through anticipation we internalize a sense of society which tacitly and invisibly controls our behavior.

In a narrower political vein, anticipated reactions frequently occur among top level policy-makers. Every member of the Canadian elite, for example, tacitly accepts that there are limits upon Canada's flexibility and maneuverability resulting from the country's juxtaposition to and interdependence with the United States. Prime Minister Trudeau spoke of the hazards of "living next to an elephant." Canadian foreign policy—and much domestic policy as well—must be understood in the context of the vast tacit influence and tacit power of the elephant to the south.

15.    Goffman, *Interaction Ritual*, p. 36. (Emphasis added.) Note that even the pronouns used in interaction affect and reflect deference, social status, etc. See Roger Brown *et al.*, "The Pronouns of Solidarity and Status" in *Psycholinguistics* (New York: Free Press, 1970).

# 2

# *Authority and Resistance*

Antoine de Saint-Exupéry's delightful children's book *The Little Prince* is full of wise, witty insights that even adults can understand. The treatment of authority is particularly instructive. In the course of his tour of the universe, the little prince pays a visit to "asteroid 325," whose sole inhabitant is a majestic king.*

"Ah! Here is a subject," exclaimed the king, when he saw the little prince coming.

And the little prince asked himself:

"How could he recognize me when he had never seen me before?"

He did not know how the world is simplified for kings. To them, all men are subjects.

"Approach, so that I may see you better," said the king, who felt consumingly proud of being at last a king over somebody.

The little prince looked everywhere to find a place to sit down; but the entire planet was crammed and obstructed by the king's magnificent ermine robe. So he remained standing upright, and, since he was tired, he yawned.

"It is contrary to etiquette to yawn in the presence of a king," the monarch said to him. "I forbid you to do so."

---

* The excerpt from *The Little Prince* by Antoine de Saint Exupéry is reprinted by permission of Harcourt Brace Jovanovich, Inc.

"I can't help it. I can't stop myself," replied the little prince, thoroughly embarrassed. "I have come on a long journey, and I have had no sleep. . . ."

"Ah, then," the king said. "I order you to yawn. It is years since I have seen anyone yawning. Yawns, to me, are objects of curiosity. Come, now! Yawn again! It is an order."

"That frightens me . . . I cannot, any more . . ." murmurmured the little prince, now completely abashed.

"Hum! Hum!" replied the king. "Then I order you sometimes to yawn and sometimes to—"

He sputtered a little, and seemed vexed.

For what the king fundamentally insisted upon was that his authority should be respected. He tolerated no disobedience. He was an absolute monarch. But, because he was a very good man, he made his orders reasonable.

"If I ordered a general," he would say, by way of example, "if I ordered a general to change himself into a sea bird, and if the general did not obey me, that would not be the fault of the general. It would be my fault."

Later, the king philosophically comments:

"One must require from each one the duty which each one can perform. . . . Accepted authority rests first of all on reason. If you ordered your people to go and throw themselves into the sea, they would rise up in revolution. I have the right to require obedience, because my orders are reasonable."

Saint-Exupéry's king can teach us a great deal about authority. The first lesson is best conveyed, however, by the unforgettable illustration of the encounter between the little prince and the king. The king is pictured in a long, flowing ermine robe which virtually encircles his tiny asteroid. He holds a scepter in his hand, and is seated majestically on a huge throne. In nearly every setting in which it is found, authority surrounds itself with symbols designed to inspire admiration and awe. Charles Merriam[1] aptly calls these symbols "miranda" (literally, "things to be admired"). The effec-

1.  Charles E. Merriam, *Political Power* (New York: Collier Books, 1964). (Originally published in 1934.)

tiveness of these miranda, however, is uncertain. Like prestige and beauty, their reality is "in the eyes of the beholder." (The little prince was *not* very impressed.) Thus, authority seeks to inculcate respect for the "miranda" to the point in some societies where a "cult" of authority is established. But even the mildest regime concerns itself to some extent with the propagation and enhancement of the miranda of authority.

Second, the mood of authority is distinctive: instead of the hypothetical or contingent form of communication characteristic of power and influence, authority expresses itself in the categorical or imperative. The king neither bargained nor pleaded with his adorable subject—he *ordered* him to yawn. Not wishing to "lose his authority," the king later modified his order, but he steadfastly avoided switching from the categorical (Do X) to either the power hypothetical (If you do X, I will do Y) or the influence hypothetical (If you do X, you will feel Y). The king gave orders. Moreover he insisted that he had a *right* to do so (because he was king). More significantly, he also insisted that he had a right to be obeyed.

Who, besides Saint-Exupéry's king, uses authority language successfully? Probably everyone. As parents we "tell our children what to do" (and what not to do). As voters we "authorise" the election of certain representatives and occasionally the approval or disapproval through referenda on specific legislation. As customers we "order" goods, service, or food. As bosses we give "instructions" to our subordinates. As husbands we (used to?) "make decisions" for the family.

A whole culture of responses to authority can be detected. Children are told that they should "be seen and not heard"; and they are warned against "talking back" to their parents. (In many respects children are at the bottom of society's language hierarchy. Yet, partially in imitation of parents and adults, they too use authority language. We all know "bossy" children. There are touches of pathos and irony in their imitative use of authority language directed toward pets and dolls. We see and hear ourselves mirrored in them. The image may be rather unattractive.) Legislators profess to believe that "the people are sovereign." Employees learn not to "question" the boss. Wives (used to?) promise in their wedding vows to "love, honor, and *obey*" their husbands. (This concept of paternal authority is rapidly dissolving, however. Perhaps representative of one trend is the case of the husband who explains that he and his wife have "divided up" the authority to make decisions. "She makes all the small decisions: where we will live, how much money we'll spend on what, where the kids go to school, etc. *I* make the *big* decisions: whether to increase defense expenditures, who should be Secretary of State, etc.")

It is occasionally possible to exercise authority (despite otherwise insurmountable linguistic barriers) simply by "acting the part." Two friends of mine traveled by ship to Greece. Immediately after the passengers disembarked, a chaotic scene developed at dockside. No one seemed to know where to go to pick up luggage, obtain ground transportation, and so forth. The passengers spoke different languages, but my friends were the only Anglophones. One of them decided to "take charge." He moved decisively to the edge of the dock, held up his arm, and said in an authoritative voice, "All those who consider themselves idiots, line up over here." To his delight, the confused passengers obediently formed a queue.

In short, authority language is used daily by nearly everyone, in situations that vary across a wide spectrum of human relationships. But some uses of authority language have far greater consequences than others. When our hen-pecked husband makes "authoritative" decisions about defense expenditures, nothing happens. When the chief executive of a "super power" makes similar decisions, billions of dollars change hands and the lives of thousands of people are affected. The words may be the same—it is the context that differs. The exercise of authority by officials high up in an organizational hierarchy reverberates throughout the entire structure. The exercise of authority by a customer in a restaurant probably affects only the waiter and the chef.

In Chapter 1 we pointed out that power sometimes takes the form of the categorical (which we have said is characteristic of authority), for example, when an armed robber demands "Give me your money." But in these situations the categorical form disguises a hypothetical meaning: "If you don't give me your money, I'll blow out your brains." Similarly, as Hobbes recognized over three centuries ago, influence sometimes assumes the categorical form, but this should not mask important differences between influence ("counsel") and authority ("command"):

> *Command* is where a man saith, *do this,* or *do not this,* without expecting other reason than the will of him that says it. . . . *Counsel* is where a man saith, *do,* or *do not this,* and deduceth his reasons from the benefit that arriveth by it to him to whom he saith it [*Leviathan,* Chapter 25].

Hobbes confuses, however, the question of meaning and intention. Counsel, unlike command, presents a hypothetical outcome as its justification. But counselors may nevertheless display self-interest in addition to, or in place of, "the benefit" of those they counsel.

The distinctive feature of authority is that the categorical form[2] cannot be reduced to a hypothetical equivalent without thereby transforming authority into either power or influence. The robber *demands*; an authority *commands*. This does not mean, however, that authorities never rely on either influence or power. But they do so because their authority has "failed" or because they prefer not to use it.

Those in positions of authority often choose not to assert it. Saint-Exupéry's king is exceptional in this regard: he could be accused of "throwing around his authority" to the point of appearing "imperious." To avoid a reputation for "heavy-handed-

---

2. Sometimes an impersonal passive construction is preferred. A sign in the local ice cream parlor insists that "Ice Cream cones and other small items *are to be* eaten outside in order to leave the tables available." This construction gives the comforting impression that the cones, not the customers, are being "bossed around."

ness," superiors tend to use the language of influence—polite request, suggestion, encouragement, etc., in preference to the categorical assertion of authority, especially when dealing with high-ranking subordinates. Since, however, subordinates usually learn that a "suggestion" from the boss is not to be taken lightly, the distinction may be more in manners than mood. By the same token the failure of influence may occasion a confrontation in which the superior asserts his authority, typically through a positive response to the subordinate's question "Is that an order?"

Individuals who are in an institutional position to use the language of authority, i.e., to issue commands, orders, directives, etc., to their "subordinates," can usually *also* use the languages of power and influence. They can "threaten" to fire a subordinate, "promise" to recommend him for a promotion, or "convince" him that a certain policy will bring good results. Thus "underlying" their authority is both power and influence, which can be used as alternatives to authority or as ways of securing compliance if the use of authoritative language "fails."

Indeed, the connotations of the term *authority* indicate its relationship to power and influence. In everyday language, one use of the word *authority,* in the sense that "A is an authority . . . ," seems to imply influence. We assume that A's statements on a certain matter should be accorded a great deal of respect precisely because A will be able to back up his statements with sound argument. In short, A's authority rests on his ability to give reasoned elaborations that prove (or at least corroborate) his statements. His influence (and his status as "an authority") would vanish if A repeatedly uttered egregiously incorrect statements about subjects in the field of his supposed expertise.

Another use of the word, in the sense that "A is *authorized* to . . . ," implies power, or, more precisely, potential power. For here authority means that A has access to some specified sanction which he is empowered to manipulate. (Or, in other words, A has been given control over some sanction.)

The definitive *Oxford English Dictionary* similarly divides its

half a page of definitions of authority into two major categories
that parallel the above distinction between the "influence-" and
the "power-" connotations of authority. The first set of definitions
focuses on the interpretation of authority in terms of the capacity
"to enforce obedience"; the second set of definitions elucidates
authority as the capacity "to influence action, opinion, belief . . ."; in more detail, ". . . title to influence the opinions of
others; authoritative opinion; weight of judgment or opinion, intellectual influence. . . ."

Almost universally, title to political authority simultaneously
entails both power and influence. Power is present because political authority provides itself with a "backing" of sanctions, both
positive and negative.[3] At the same time, however, the application

3. Many theorists have placed undue emphasis on the negative sanctions,
thereby distracting attention from the perhaps equally important positive sanctions that nearly all governments manipulate. (Cf. Max
Weber's definition of government as being characterized by a monopo-
listic claim to the legitimate use of coercion.) Emphasis on negative
sanctions is inappropriate even in describing the authority structures
of "primitive" tribes. Among the Nambikwara Indians, for example,
an "autocracy" obtains, but Claude Lévi-Strauss takes great pains to
show how "slender" is the authority of the chief. Despite the importance of his position, the chief lacks entirely the "powers of
coercion." Instead he is limited to the use of positive sanctions: "the
first and main instrument of his power is his generosity. . . ." He
must have under his control "surplus quantities of food, tools, weapons, and ornaments which, however trifling in themselves, are nonetheless considerable in relation to the prevailing poverty." While his
power base is therefore quite small, his influence base is considerably
larger. "Personal prestige and the ability to inspire confidence" are
the foundations of authority in Nambikwara society. The chief must
be possessed of ingenuity and knowledge of the territories such that
his decisions and opinions will be respected. But his decisions are not
made in a despotical vacuum. Instead he appears in the guise of "a
politician struggling to maintain an uncertain majority." The ultimate
arbiter of any major conflict is public opinon, however imperfectly
determined. And, most significantly, the giving of consent precedes
and accompanies the existence of authority. Despite the privileges (including the right to polygamy) granted to the chief, in part to help
alleviate the burdens of his office, he is nonetheless obligated to per-

of sanctions is usually delimited by a set of explicit or implicit norms that stipulate the conditions under which sanctions may be applied. The use of a particular sanction must be "justifiable" in terms of these norms. In other words, just as the "expert" authority must be able to elaborate upon his statements in such a way as to corroborate them, so the "political" authority must be prepared to elaborate upon the reasons behind his actions or decisions in order to "justify" them should his authority be called into question. Saint-Exupéry's king insisted that he had a "right" to be obeyed, because his orders were "reasonable."

But in what sense may orders and other so-called "authoritative" communications be described as "reasonable"? What are the grounds for reasoning in support of such claims for authority? And why would anyone accept such reasoning or obey the orders that rest upon it?

This question forces us to examine the articles of faith and belief that surround authority and serve to legitimize its exercise. (Merriam calls these the *credenda,* literally, "things to be believed.") The following typology of credenda is based upon Max Weber's famous analysis of authority.[4]

| TYPE OF AUTHORITY | BELIEF SYSTEMS SUPPORTING AUTHORITY (CREDENDA) |
|---|---|
| | *Nature of Belief* |
| *Charismatic* | Belief that an individual (usually) or group is endowed with supernatural or superhuman abilities to make good decisions for a collectivity. |

form certain functions for the tribe as a whole. Thus the relationship between chief and tribe is one of reciprocity, "a constantly adjusted equilibrium of oaths and privileges, services and responsibilities." Claude Lévi-Strauss, *Tristes Tropiques.* Tr. by John Russell. (New York: Atheneum, 1971), pp. 302–10.

4.  See Max Weber, "The Social Psychology of World Religions" in Hans Gerth and C. Wright Mills, eds., *From Max Weber* (New York: Oxford University Press, 1958), pp. 259ff.

| TYPE OF AUTHORITY | BELIEF SYSTEMS SUPPORTING AUTHORITY (CREDENDA) |
|---|---|

### Source of Belief

*Religious:* a) Scripture, or some personal characteristic or deed that appears to fulfill scriptural prophecy.

b) Some magical event or events in which God or deities appear to have designated the charismatic ruler (i.e., a "sign").

*Secular:* a) Unusual ability or capacity, often demonstrated in seemingly irrelevant arenas (e.g., sports, academe, etc.).

b) Personal attractiveness, "sex appeal," etc.[5]

### Nature of Belief

*Traditional*

A certain form of rule "has always existed" or has "been around for a long time" and is therefore to be preferred to innovations that are "untested." By the same token, traditional authority may be closely circumscribed by "ancient" substantive and procedural constraints in the form of customs and "traditional practices."

### Source of Belief

Custom, habit, superstition, religious conviction, etc.

5. The contemporary tendency to equate "charisma" with "sex appeal" represents a lamentable dilution of the original Weberian meaning of the term. It is included here with the caveat that true "charisma" is a rare commodity indeed. A compromise definition of charisma might be "unusual and attractive abilities."

| TYPE OF AUTHORITY | BELIEF SYSTEMS SUPPORTING AUTHORITY (CREDENDA) |
|---|---|

### Nature of Belief

*Rational-Legal*  The existing system embodies at the highest level norms of efficiency, effectiveness, etc. (technological rationality) which are protected by certain constitutional or statutory guarantees (legality) affecting both the substance of decisions and the procedures followed in selecting those who occupy positions of authority.

### Source of Belief

Sophisticated indoctrination, usually presupposing widespread literacy and the growth of bureaucracy as both cause and effect of the entire system.

While Weber himself recognized that the usefulness of his classification could "only be judged by its results in promoting systematic analysis," and furthermore that none of his "three ideal types . . . is usually to be found in historical cases in 'pure' form . . . ," the concepts do promote interesting analysis of both "dynamic" (or developmental) and "static" considerations. Developmentally, Weber's idealizations serve as categories into which historical examples can be placed according to the element of authority that is predominant in a given case. Viewed historically, and despite important exceptions, one can say that authority has evolved from the "traditional" to the "rational-legal" form, with "charismatic" interludes often characterizing societies that have had a revolutionary history.[6]

Within any one epoch of development, Weber's categories

6. For a brilliantly succinct description of the evolution of credenda in Western society, see R. M. MacIver's chapter "The Firmament of Law" in *The Web of Government,* 2nd ed. (New York: Free Press, 1965). The quotations from Weber can be found in his *Theory of Social and Economic Organization,* Talcott Parsons, ed. (New York: Free Press, 1964), pp. 328–29.

help us identify different aspects of authority. Thus the authority of the American President, while predominantly based on respect for the "legality" of the Constitution and belief in the "rationality" of the system as a whole, depends as well on the personal "charisma" of the man who happens to occupy the office of the President; and on the habitual patterns of deference and obedience that over the past two centuries have become "traditional" with respect to the office.[7] One can only speculate to what exent the Watergate crisis has "weakened" the authority of the President by disturbing these habitual patterns.

Besides Weber's trichotomy, there are other ways to categorize the credenda of authority. For example, some beliefs about authority emphasize questions of *procedure* (i.e., how rulers are chosen, how decisions are reached, etc.), whereas others stress considerations of *substance.* Substantive legitimacy (a doctrine typified in Plato's *Republic*) accords acceptance to a ruler on the basis not of how he is chosen, or how he arrives at and implements his decisions, but rather on the basis of the quality of his acts and decisions themselves. Thus, for example, any ruler who "abuses" authority by using it to serve his private ends rather than the "public good" is a "tyrant" (i.e., an illegitimate ruler). The idea of "public good," moreover, is fixed, static, and (given proper education) discernible, like the other "pure forms," truth, beauty, justice, etc.

Notions of substantive legitimacy can be traced through medieval thought (Aquinas argued that the ruler's action must accord with "natural law" as interpreted by the Church) and even down to and beyond Machiavelli's political theory. Perhaps the "purest" exponent of substantive legitimacy, Machiavelli openly

7. Another student of Weber, Seymour Martin Lipset, has attempted to interpret the evolution of the Presidency as a case of George Washington's charismatic leadership gradually becoming "routinized" through the process of selecting and legitimizing various successors. See Lipset, *The First New Nation* (New York: Basic Books, 1963). "Routinization of charisma" is discussed in Weber, *Theory of Social and Economic Organization,* pp. 363–86.

counseled the use of "evil means" to achieve authority that would then be legitimized by the performance of "good deeds." (In a sense Machiavelli was not the antithesis but the fulfillment of Plato in this regard.)

English liberal thought as embodied in the writings of John Locke also adopted a substantive view of legitimacy. The ruler's prerogative to be obeyed operated so long as he did not abuse authority repeatedly and with a "general design" of "enslaving" the people. Likewise Hobbes explicitly asserts that the "sovereign," regardless of how he acquired authority—i.e., by convention or by conquest—is legitimate so long as he acts to maintain order and protect the members of society.

The first significant deviation from substantive legitimacy theory toward a concept of "procedural" legitimacy occurred in the writings of Jean Jacques Rousseau. For the doctrine that a ruler's actions are legitimate so long as they are not "tyrannical" in substance, Rousseau substituted the idea of the "general will": acts of the sovereign derive their legitimacy from the way in which the decision to perform the act was reached. In other words, "the people" do not delegate power to representatives (or other agents) who are then sovereign within certain predetermined substantive limits; rather, the people retain sovereignty and agree to legitimize only those actions arrived at through the *procedure* of the general will.

In a sense, Rousseau merely took Locke's idea of "popular sovereignty" to its logical conclusion and converted it from a negative concept (in which the people could *withdraw* support from a "tyrant") to a positive one (in which the people actually participated in decision-making and rulership). But Rousseau's formulation was strenuously resisted in England for more than a century. During this time, however, the notion of Parliamentary sovereignty gradually superseded the earlier notion of mixed sovereignty, i.e., separation of power among Commons, Lords, and King. This in turn made possible the transition from the medieval notion of substantive legitimacy to a kind of *de facto* Rousseauian procedural legitimacy. Involved in this evolutionary transition were two changes: (a) the concentration of legislative authority in the lower house of Parliament, and (b) the democratization of Parliament. Once these changes had taken place, procedural legitimacy almost totally supplanted substantive legitimacy with the result that virtually any law duly enacted by Parliament today would be "constitutional" and "authoritative."

American developments paralleled the British pattern, but some interesting differences occurred. For one thing, the change in the doctrine of legitimacy was not evolutionary but revolutionary. Thus, it was accomplished more quickly and dramatically, and yet less completely, than in Britain. The leaders of the American Revolution opposed British policy on the grounds that the *substance* of the Acts made them illegitimate on their face. The various British Acts promulgated between 1763 and 1776, they argued, amounted to a "system of slavery." But the revolutionaries also developed an embryonic theory of procedural legitimacy manifested in the cry, "No taxation without representation." Thus, notions of *both* substantive and procedural legitimacy played a part in the philosophy of the American Revolution.

The break with British authority accomplished by the successful Declaration of Independence necessitated the development of a new theory of legitimacy to replace the old one that had been destroyed. Strict conformity to the radical "democratic" Rousseauian model would have dictated that legitimacy be placed on a purely procedural basis. But the Americans were reluctant (for a variety of reasons) to abandon entirely the substantive notion embodied in Lockeian philosophy. They doubted the efficacy of purely procedural (i.e., "democratic") constraints on rulers, and insisted on prescribing significant substantive limits to the exercise of power. In at least this one sense, therefore, the Founding Fathers demonstrated a profound distrust of democracy. Furthermore, they transmitted to later generations a legacy of substantive limitations on authority exemplified in the practice of judicial review and the doctrine that certain types of decision could be declared "unconstitutional" regardless of the procedures followed in taking them. In practice, the application of substantive limitations in United States politics is complicated by institutional arrangements that make the President independent of the day-to-day "confidence" of Congress, while leaving the Supreme Court pretty much dependent on Executive support to implement its decisions. Had Watergate occurred in Britain (or probably Canada) the political career of the man responsible would likely have ended abruptly.

Robert Dahl outlines yet another typology of the credenda of authority in his *After the Revolution?*, the subtitle of which is "Authority in a Good Society." According to Dahl, acceptance of authority may rest on the belief that:

1) the relevant process insures "that decisions correspond with my *personal choice* . . ." or
2) the process insures "decisions informed by a special *competence* that would be less likely under alternative procedures . . ." or finally
3) the process may be preferred "because it *economizes on* the amount of *time,* attention and energy I must give to it. . . ." [8]

The diversity of these various credenda serves to illustrate my central point, namely, that credenda are *conventional.* This view contradicts the notion that authority is somehow "natural," that we automatically accept it because it is part of human nature. Some sort of hierarchy may be instinctive or natural (many higher animals generate hierarchies or "pecking orders"); the specific

8. Robert Dahl, *After the Revolution* (New Haven: Yale University Press, 1970), p. 8. Note that all of his criteria for accepting authority stress process and procedure almost to the exclusion of substantive concerns. In this respect Dahl appears more European than American. For a critique (by a European) of the modern trend to abandon substantive limitations on authority in favor of procedural ones, see Bertrand de Jouvenel, *Sovereignty: An Enquiry Into the Public Good* (Cambridge: At The University Press, 1957).

form, and indeed the rich vicissitudes of credenda and miranda, certainly are not.

For a long time, however, it was assumed that hierarchical roles were somehow "natural": people were "born" into them. The implication of this view is starkly clear: one's position in life was fixed from birth, ascribed from the moment of first consciousness.[9] Furthermore, authority relationships were viewed as general rather than as specific. One's superior was superior in every respect and in every social context.

Centuries ago, many people believed that authority descended from God, and thus human resistance to authority was tantamount to heresy or sacrilege, a rejection of God's will. Competing with the "descending" interpretation of authority, however, was its antithesis, the view that authority ascended from the ruled to the ruler. In this perspective, authority was granted on the condition that the ruler fulfill certain criteria, including procedural considerations related to how he should be chosen (for example, by election, by inheritance through the male line) and substantive considerations outlining what his authority did (and did not) allow him to do. Rulers who abrogated the procedural norms were called usurpers or tyrants "without a title" (*sine titulo*). Rulers who repudiated substantive limitations on their authority also earned the designation of tyrant, *ab exercitio,* indicating a questioning only of their exercise of, and not their title to, authority.

The emergence of "modernity" involved a change in the perception of authority and a gradual replacement of "descending" credenda by various versions of the "ascending" thesis. Social status and position in the authority structure became, ideally at least, a function of individual achievement rather than of social ascription. Instead of a title to general dominance, moreover, the

9. One version of this cosmogony, particularly evident in several medieval philosophies, interpreted the entire universe in terms of a hierarchical metaphor resembling a "great chain of being." See Arthur Lovejoy, *The Great Chain of Being* (Cambridge, Mass.: Harvard University Press, 1936).

authority of superiors (again ideally) came to be seen as limited to specific spheres of competence. A prominent exception, of course, is the "totalitarian" doctrine of the state (e.g., Hitler's or Mussolini's) which claims absolute and total authority over the individual. Generally, however, the ideology of modernity was expressed in terms of achievement and specificity.

Even more important than the postulation of "modern" ideals was the recognition that authority relations are not inbred or genetically determined but instead constitute a part of "learned behavior." The child does not automatically accept the authority of the parent, as anyone familiar with small children will readily testify. Someone must ingrain habits of obedience in children through what is innocuously termed the "socialization process," using techniques that range from subtle psychological manipulation to overt compulsion—from persuasion to bribery to force. Children are first taught they "must" obey Mother and Father. Later they learn to obey Teacher. In their games they learn "to play by the rules," a concept later translated into the imperative of "obeying" the law. Indeed, much of the socialization process is intended to prepare the way for the acceptance of authority in different spheres, including "the political."

Thus, to understand the habit of obedience we must turn attention to the techniques of socialization. Our analysis relies in part on the concepts of power and influence elaborated in Chapter 1, but the inventory of motivations which will be advanced to "explain" obedience should be regarded as illustrative rather than exhaustive. The distinguished political sociologist R. M. MacIver sagely advised that "no history of specific motivations" can account adequately for the phenomenon of obedience: "All the ties that hold men together in any society, all the needs and all the hopes that depend on their society for realization, prompt them to law-abidingness." [10]

10.  MacIver, *The Web of Government*, p. 59. In a little noticed paragraph at the beginning of his discussion of the three types of authority, Weber similarly warned against reliance on a single explanation of

## "LEARNING" THE CREDENDA OF AUTHORITY

Learning patterns with respect to the credenda that legitimize authority probably vary according to the "type" of authority; hence generalizations across these types are next to impossible. The manner in which one learns to accept charismatic authority, for instance, would likely differ considerably from the learning of traditional or rational-legal authority: it could take the form of an instantaneous "conversion" to "true belief." No doubt the best written account of the complex psychological and emotional aspects of such an experience would be found in appropriate autobiographical accounts. Despite similarities, each experience would in many important respects appear idiosyncratic.

How does one learn to accept traditional authority? In its literal sense, such learning results from the "handing down" to new generations of reverence for the beliefs and values of the past. But conscious articulation of this process is likely to occur only when it comes under severe attack. A case in point is Edmund Burke's *Reflections on the Revolution in France.* The traditionalist conservatism which Burke so devoutly espoused was articulated only with great misgivings about the very act of writing his reflections, and only under the profound threat he felt the "metaphysic sophistry" of the French revolutionaries posed to his values. Burke undoubtedly speaks for all true (traditional) conservatives in his admission that "we are alarmed into reflection."

Tradition, however, plays a part in the institutionalization of all types of authority practices and relationships. The very passage of time provides a new basis for the acceptance of authority

---

the mystery of civil obedience. After listing several motives for obeying a superior, including "custom, . . . affective ties, . . . a purely material complex of interests, or . . . ideal (*wertrational*) motives . . . ," Weber introduced, as "a further element" that is "normally" present, the typology of beliefs in legitimacy upon which most of his students focus their exclusive attention. *Theory of Social and Economic Organizations,* p. 325.

by "hallowing" the relationship in the reverence due old age. Often, however, the "original" meaning is lost, so to speak, in translation. The conventions established by the "first generation" may have appeared quite differently, and indeed far more rational, than the inherited routines passed along to succeeding generations often as "empty" rituals. Many religious taboos exemplify this transformation. Once important for sanitary reasons, the ban on eating certain types of food today appears "irrational." But it is nonetheless "authoritative." Through formal and informal teaching, these practices (and many others) get passed along from generation to generation, acquiring legitimacy in part because of their age.

Finally we turn to the learning of rational legal authority. Here social scientists have done a great deal more homework. A recent survey of the literature on "political socialization" identified the following institutions as important socializing agents: family, peer groups, the school system, social groupings (i.e., based on class, race, ethnicity, etc.), and secondary political groups such as political parties.[11] The political learning process can be divided into three stages. Very young children in stage 1 have quite idealized—usually positive and uncritical—images of authority. Only later on do children develop an awareness of authority as a conventional political institution (stage 2). Later still is the recognition that as an adult member of the community, the citizen has a right to participate in the making of decisions (stage 3).

If indeed we accept the model of the three stages of orientation toward authority—submissive, accountable, and participatory[12]—then it is remarkable the extent to which large numbers

11.  Richard Dawson and Kenneth Prewitt, *Political Socialization* (Boston: Little, Brown, 1969).
     (Note: I have assumed that studies such as those on which Dawson and Prewitt base their conclusions can be classified as case studies of rational-legal authority.)
12.  A similar model has been applied to a cross-national study of the stages of development of entire political cultures, classifying them as "parochial," "subject," and "civic." Republished in the same series

of citizens, even in what purports to be the most "advanced" society in the world, have remained fixated at stage 1. In an experiment—repeated many times under varying conditions—designed to test the willingness of human subjects to administer painful shocks to fellow human beings "under orders," Stanley Milgram found a surprising receptivity to authority. The experiment, which underwent numerous variations and modifications, was disguised as a "learning test" for the "victim," who in fact was part of the research team. The "executant" was the true subject. He was "instructed" (always in "authority language" but in varying contexts) to administer increasingly severe shocks each time the victim answered incorrectly a question from a (fake) learning test. Realistic moans, sobs, and pleas could be heard coming from the testing booth. Despite this feedback (which ceased ominously after a certain threshold of voltage) and in utter disregard of a prominently displayed danger sign near the maximum voltage indicator, a frighteningly large percentage of the subjects continued to administer shocks to the maximum. Most would have gone on to even higher voltages had that been possible. In a masterpiece of understatement, Milgram commented in dismay, "Perhaps our culture does not provide adequate models for disobedience." [13]

Milgram's subjects were all adults, already "fully socialized" to certain ideas about authority. Jean Piaget reached rather different conclusions about socialization by studying responses to authority among children. In the belief that authority and justice are related to one another, Piaget tried to find out under what conditions children would choose obedience to authority over fidelity to their notions of fairness and justice. Piaget's researchers told children of different ages stories in which an "unfair" situa-

as Dawson and Prewitt, this study bears the title *The Civic Culture.* See G. Almond and S. Verba, *The Civic Culture* (Princeton: Princeton University Press, 1963).

13. Stanley Milgram, "Some Conditions of Obedience and Disobedience to Authority," *Human Relations,* 18, fall 1965. See also Milgram's *Obedience to Authority* (New York: Harper and Row, 1973).

tion would be authorized or supported by some authority figure
(e.g., an adult, a father). The children were then asked to comment on the situation portrayed in the story, and particularly to
indicate whether the assertion of authority should be accepted or
resisted.

Piaget's findings were slightly more encouraging than Milgram's, although we do not know whether he had a very representative sample of children. In any event, Piaget found a close
relationship between age and tendency to *question* authority. Very
young children tended to accept without hesitation authority that
was contrary to their notion of fairness. Older children adopted a
more critical and uncooperative posture, often resisting authority
they regarded as unjust. It would seem, therefore, that the children
in the eight to eleven years age group had at least advanced to
stage 2 of the Dawson/Prewitt scale of political learning. Whether
the Milgram experiment shows that a regression back to an earlier
stage occurs once people get outside the school system,[14] or
whether it rather reflects the backwardness of American political
culture when contrasted with that of Switzerland and France
(where Piaget did his work), is impossible to determine on the
basis of these data. One can safely conclude that learning about

---

14. We must be careful to avoid the assumption that learning ends in
    public school. On the contrary, the most significant *political* learning
    takes place during middle and late adolescence. Furthermore, such
    notorious institutions as boot camp accomplish with surprising suc-
    cess important training with respect to authority. The concept of dis-
    cipline refers to the automatic, almost reflex obedience which basic
    training attempts to inculcate. Interestingly, some military personnel
    have begun to relax discipline in the realization that young recruits in
    the 1970's are incorrigibly antiauthoritarian. It has even been sug-
    gested that the United States abolished military conscription in 1973
    because conscripts were impossible to discipline. A favorite slogan,
    scrawled on washroom and barrack walls from San Francisco to
    Saigon, was FTA (fuck the army).
        For the Piaget study see Jean Piaget, *The Moral Judgment of the
    Child* (New York: The Free Press, 1956), pp. 276–95.

authority can be badly distorted to emphasize obeying authority over understanding its "reasonable" bases. The terrifyingly popular slogan, "America—Love it or Leave it!" obviously belongs at the level of stage 1.

The psychologist L. Kohlberg has outlined an even more elaborate scale of cognitive-moral development concerning concepts of authority and justice. Kohlberg goes beyond the procedurally oriented Dawson/Prewitt approach to indicate as well the substance of moral development. His six stages are as follows:

1. Obedience and punishment orientation (authoritarianism)
2. Self-satisfaction (pleasure principle)
3. Conformity to majority rule
4. Law and order
5. Social contract
6. Universality and consistency.

Interestingly, Kohlberg found that only 13 per cent of all subjects below stage 6 on this scale refused to collaborate with Milgram, but 75 per cent of those at stage 6 "resisted" the "authority" of Milgram's experimenters.[15]

While we have avoided presenting in this section a full-blown theory of learning with respect to political legitimacy, the emphasis has been to show that political socialization, insofar as it shapes feelings and beliefs about authority, affects the willingness of individuals to accept authority. But implicitly, we have thereby indicated the possibility of learning "illegitimacy," so to speak. Such learning is not to be treated lightly. In the words of Christian Bay, although "most of us have become trained, as generations of our ancestors, to obey all laws almost by instinct, and certainly by habit, if not by conviction, others have become

---

15.  For a discussion of Kohlberg see William Eckhardt, *Compassion* (Oakville, Ont.: C.P.R.I., 1972), ch. 6. I am grateful to Dr. Eckhardt for communicating personally to me the cross-correlation between Milgram and Kohlberg.

conditioned to breaking laws." [16] The important thing to keep in mind is that the stark alternatives of learning to accept authority without question and learning to reject it absolutely falsely dichotomize what is surely a continuum of finely shaded alternatives. The vast majority of response dispositions would be located between the extremes of pure acceptance and pure rejection. Most members of society learn something about accepting authority but also learn, however poorly, that authority is not infallible, and that obedience is not always a divine imperative. Variation occurs respecting the sphere of authority—family, school, health, science, employment, and so forth. Habitual criminals have been known to emerge from authoritarian family backgrounds. But even within the sphere of political authority, for example, most children learn some notion of limitation upon the obligation to obey.

Reviewing our discussion so far, authority is a communications-relationship expressed as an order or command. Although there may be sanctions available to the "author" of this communication, they remain "in the distance." The command is accepted not because of the sanctions but because the command itself is viewed as "legitimate" in terms of a set of beliefs called "credenda." Individuals learn an authority "credo" through a multi-faceted process of "political socialization" which varies in substance if not technique according to the types of authority: traditional, charismatic, and rational-legal. In theory, "pure" authority is always "successful." The subject assumes that the command issued by an authority is capable of "reasoned elaboration" in accordance with the credenda, and thus he obeys automatically. In practice, it is difficult to know precisely what role the belief in legitimacy plays in the overall complex of possible motivations for obedience. This brings us to the problem of the "failure" of authority.

16.  Christian Bay, "Civil Disobedience: Prerequisite for Democracy in Mass Society," in Donald W. Hanson and Robert B. Fowler, eds., *Obligation and Dissent* (Boston: Little, Brown, 1971).

CRISES AND BREAKDOWNS IN AUTHORITY

While authority is theoretically characterized by the capacity for "reasoned elaboration" of its commands and orders, the definitional link between authority and legitimacy makes it almost impossible to separate the objective basis for authority from the subjective perception that it exists (legitimacy). Furthermore, attention to the teaching and learning of legitimacy illustrates the extent to which perceptions are malleable. Children (and adults as well) can "learn" to regard as "legitimate" regimes whose supposed authority rests on little other than the partial control of the agents of socialization.

Even if the analysis of credenda were freed of these complications, we would still be troubled by the difficulty of deciding ultimately what "motivates" people to obey authority. Realizing that authorities almost always "possess" (potential) power and influence, how can we be sure that obedience is not simply a kind of "anticipated reaction" in response to the power or influence that underlies authority? In other words, when does authority really work as authority?

Apart from literally reading the mind of everyone subject to authority to find out whether in this particular instance obedience occurs because of the belief that the given exercise of authority is legitimate in terms of the prevailing credenda or whether some other motivation (e.g., fear of the consequences of disobeying) is the predominant concern, we have no way of knowing. But there is at least a *prima facie* "test" of authority in the phenomenon of obedience itself. So long as orders and commands are accepted "automatically," so long as laws (the impersonal expression of authority) are obeyed, in short, as long as the language of authority "works" and authorities do not have to "resort" to influence or power language, we may assume that authority is functioning. Indeed, some writers insist that such a *de facto* approach is the only way to define authority. Felix Oppenheim, for example, declares that:

> Those in political power normally succeed in securing compliance with their decisions simply because they possess authority. That is because the subjects . . . have formed the habit of considering official enactments to have binding force, regardless of whether they approve of them.[17]

A similar *de facto* approach is embodied in Weber's definition of "imperative control" (*Herrschaft*) as "the probability that a command with a given specific content will be obeyed by a given group of persons." [18] In the same vein, Herbert Simon defines authority as:

> . . . a relationship between two individuals, one "superior," the other "subordinate." The superior frames and transmits decisions with the expectation that they will be obeyed by the subordinate. The subordinate expects such decisions, and his conduct is determined by them.
>
> The relationship of authority can be defined, therefore, in purely objective and behavioristic terms. . . . When the behaviors [described above] do not occur there is no authority, whatever may be the "paper" theory of organization.[19]

The *de facto* concept of authority, despite its limitations, helps highlight the fascinating phenomenon of "breakdown" of

17.  Felix Oppenheim, *Dimensions of Freedom* (New York: St. Martin's Press, 1961), p. 32.
18.  Weber, *Theory of Economic and Social Organizations,* p. 152. Immediately following this sentence is a qualification suggesting that habitual obedience is a subset of authority, for Weber introduces the term "discipline" to refer to "the probability that by virtue of habituation a command will receive prompt and automatic obedience. . . ." Later he elaborates on the concept of discipline, stating that it includes the "habituation characteristic of uncritical and unresisting mass obedience" (p. 153). Presumably, there are forms of authority in which obedience to commands and orders falls short of being uncritical and unresisting; at this point Weber's three types of legitimation would become relevant.
19.  Herbert Simon, *Administrative Behavior,* 2nd ed. (New York: Free Press, 1957), p. 125.

authority in a situation of "crisis." We subject our earlier hypothesis about how authority "works" to a valuable negative test by examining circumstances in which authority repeatedly fails.

When individuals begin to "question" authority, a crisis in authority is just around the corner. For despite the pretense that authority is reasonable and therefore justifiable, in practice authority (at least in large-scale organizations like the modern state) relies on automatic acceptance. We may treat this as a paradox of roughly the same proportions as "catch-22." In his tremendously popular World War II novel, author Joseph Heller explains how the Air Force effectively prevented the grounding of "crazy" flyers despite the existence of a rule stipulating that crazy flyers must be grounded. There was of course a catch. The rule stipulated that a crazy flyer must be grounded, but first he must *ask* to be grounded for reasons of insanity. But according to catch-22, "Anyone who wants to get out of combat duty isn't really crazy."

Applied to a particular flyer named Orr, catch-22 worked with "absolute simplicity":

> Orr was crazy and could be grounded. All he had to do was ask; and as soon as he did, he would no longer be crazy and would have to fly more missions. Orr would be crazy to fly more missions and sane if he didn't, but if he was sane he had to fly them. If he flew them he was crazy and didn't have to; but if he didn't want to he was sane and had to.[20]

Similarly, authority is obligatory because it is capable of reasoned elaboration. But to demand that such reasoned elaboration be made explicit is to "challenge" authority.

Indeed, a major tactic of those who wish to "disrupt" authority is to demand explicit elaborations of the reasons behind authoritative communications. Imagine what would happen if every motorist approaching an intersection demanded from the traffic cop a "reasoned elaboration" of the commands to stop,

20. Joseph Heller, *Catch-22* (New York: Simon & Schuster, 1961), p. 46.

proceed, turn, etc. Such a challenge would force the policeman to change from authority to influence. An even more serious challenge such as an escaping armed robber might pose would force him to use power. In either case, the type of communication would take the "hypothetical" form rather than the "categorical" of authority. For example, a) "If you don't stop, there will be an accident at this corner"; b) "If you don't stop, I'll shoot."

We begin to approach the position that authority crises evidence "failure of socialization." But we must be careful not to mistake what may be only a symptom (i.e., failure of socialization) for real "causes" such as underlying social and political changes which make the old credenda irrelevant to new conditions. Leaving such difficulties aside, however, disobedience appears from this perspective to result either from insufficient exposure to values and beliefs supporting the authority structure; or from learning new "credenda" that contradict or undermine the prevailing ideology of authority. Indeed, revolutionaries typically propound or espouse a model for structuring and legitimizing authority relations that differs from the prevailing credenda. It was concern over precisely this source of instability that led Plato and Hobbes to insist that the state rigidly control the teaching of doctrine and opinion to prevent the spread of "subversive" ideas.[21]

But even if "subversive" ideas were eliminated, even if socialization were perfect, authority crises could still result if the authorities abused or exceeded their authority as set forth in the prevailing credenda. (This of course assumes that the credenda stopped short of legitimizing unconditionally absolute authority.) Again the question of perception is paramount: whenever a gap

---

21.  "[I]t is annexed to the sovereignty, to be judge of what opinions and doctrines are averse, and what conducing to peace; and consequently, on what occasions, how far, and what men are to be trusted withal, in speaking to multitudes of people; and who shall examine the doctrines of all books before they be published. For the actions of men proceed from their opinions; and in the well-governing of opinions, consisteth the well-governing of men's actions, in order to their peace, and concord." *Leviathan* Ch. 18.

develops between the (perceived) credenda and the perceptions of the exercise of authority, there exists the potential for an authority crisis. In general, the more sophisticated a citizenry with respect to its level of cognitive-moral development, the more elaborate its understanding of the limitations on authority, the more complete its information about the substance and procedures of authoritative decision-making, the more likely the occurrence of authority crises.

Conversely, the lower the level of cognitive development, the less inclined people are to question, or even be aware of the possibility of questioning authority; the less information available about how and what the rulers are doing, the less likely authority will be challenged. Some societies are easier to "govern" than others.

When someone makes a conscious decision not to obey authority, genuinely believing that for one of the above reasons the authority in question is illegitimate, we may speak of *resistance*. More extreme than the mere questioning of, or even protest against, authority, resistance involves a determination not to "go along" with authority. In its passive form, resistance amounts to noncooperation. In its active form, resistance may range over a wide array of strategies, from nonviolent to violent, unorganized to highly organized, individual to mass. Its focus may be limited to a specific policy or person, or generalized to the authority system as a whole.

Though by definition resistance aims at the limitation—and sometimes the utter destruction—of an authority system, the concept of resistance does not apply to all limitations on authority. Specifically excluded, for example, are the numerous institutional mechanisms and processes that are built into the machinery of government (through constitutionalism, the party system, etc.) to limit political authority. It is important to point out, however, that the introduction of institutional devices (like political parties and constitutionalism) for legal "opposition" (as opposed to illegal "resistance") is a relatively recent phenomenon in modern politics, almost always bloodied by violence, and far from universal even today. In Weber's categories, these devices mark the transition from "traditional" forms of imperative control (in which the limitations on authority were established by custom) to "legalistic" systems in which limitations are embedded in the constitutional framework.[22]

## AUTHORITY AND ORGANIZATION

So far we have explored why people obey or accept authority in terms of the beliefs (credenda) and symbols (miranda) which help sustain it. What role or function does authority fulfill? This question directs our attention to the organizational context in which authority usually operates. In the words of Herbert Simon:

> Organized behavior . . . results when each of the coordinated individuals sets for himself a criterion of choice that makes his own behavior dependent on the behavior of others. In the simplest cases he makes his own decision at each point as to what those adjustments should be. In slightly more complex forms of organization, *he sets himself a general rule which permits the communicated decision of another to guide his own choices. . . .*[23]

Communicated decisions that guide the choice of another are precisely what we mean by "authoritative communications." The simplest paradigm is "Do X"; more complex formulations still re-

22.  Application of these categories is complicated by such facts as the ancient and medieval tradition of natural and divine law as checks on a ruler's authority, the British "custom" of common law, and other traditional, implicit aspects of the so-called British constitution, etc. For a full treatment of resistance, see David V. J. Bell, *Resistance and Revolution* (Boston: Houghton Mifflin, 1973), where some of the preceding paragraphs previously appeared. J. G. A. Pocock cogently discusses the contrast between ritual and custom on the one hand, and positive law on the other as sources of authority and order. See his *Politics, Language and Time* (New York: Atheneum, 1971), especially ch. 2.

23.  Simon, *Administrative Behavior,* p. 125. (Emphasis in original.)

tain the imperative mood, whether called orders, instructions, rules, regulations, or whatever.

Authority is a mechanism *par excellence* for coordinating action among individuals. When authority is "working properly," things get done. A hierarchy of superior-subordinate relationships is established. Individuals (or subgroups) are assigned tasks, i.e., they are told what to do. This division of labor is formalized in rules or customs which lay out *procedures for taking decisions,* and also ensure that decisions reached at one level in the hierarchy will be acted upon by those "further down" responsible for implementation.

Through the mechanism of authority and the attendant division of labor large numbers of people are able to interact in a productive way to accomplish a wide range of collective activities. In coordinated action, authority can be seen as a vast improvement over either power (which may breed hostility) or influence (which is unstable). This statement should not be taken to mean that where authority is present, power and influence evaporate. On the contrary, all three tend to coexist. Authority, however, does stand out as a technique which, while "backed" by power or influence, operates in a different and in this case far more efficient manner, replacing threats/promises or persuasive arguments with "decrees," "instructions," "rules," and so on.

Moreover, authoritative communications are assumed (under "normal" conditions) to evoke automatic, predictable responses. When the boss "tells" his secretary to "take a memo," "get the Jones file," or "cancel a meeting," she "does what she is told." She may not click her heels, but she will probably say "Right away, sir." When it "works," authority is very effective and highly efficient.

To "work properly" as a mechanism for coordination, however, authority requires a) thorough indoctrination in the "standing rules" of organizational operating procedure; b) socialization of organization members to the niceties of status differentiation within the organization—the privileges and obligations attached to each position in the status hierarchy; and c) adequate communications networks and channels (corresponding to the "lines of authority") to provide a medium for the expression of authoritative decisions that constitutes the exercise of authority.

In his pioneering study of organizations, Chester Barnard distinguished between the *subjective* aspects of authority (the values and attitudes of organization members) and its *objective* aspects (lines of authority, communication channels, etc.). He presents an interesting inventory of seven "controlling factors" governing the "objective system of authority," but maintains throughout that both subjective and objective elements must be present to permit authority to exist, arguing in effect that authority exists "in the eyes of the beholder." Skillfully combining subjective with objective aspects, Barnard defines authority as:

> The character of a communication (order) in a formal organization by virtue of which it is accepted by a contributor to or "member" of the organization as governing the action he contributes. . . . [T]he decision as to whether an order has authority or not lies with the persons to whom it is addressed, and does not reside in "persons of authority" or those who issue orders.[24]

Accordingly, Barnard hypothesizes that a communication will be authoritative only if it possesses the following characteristics:

   a)   the person to whom it is addressed can and does understand it;
   b)   he believes it to be compatible with the purposes of the organization and
   c)   with his personal interests as a whole;
   d)   he is physically and mentally able to comply.

Points c and d in particular recall Saint-Exupéry's king, who similarly theorized that orders must not be clearly damaging to the interests of the individual (e.g., suicidal) or impossible to

24.   Chester Barnard, *The Functions of the Executive* (Cambridge, Mass.: Harvard University Press, 1968), p. 163. (First published in 1938.)

fulfill (e.g., metamorphosis into a sea bird). Indeed, Barnard tells us, the wise executive, like the wise king, will carefully avoid issuing an order which, because it violates one or more of the above criteria for "authoritativeness," is unlikely to be carried out. To do so would "undermine" his authority. Even in times of emergency when the "zone of acceptance" (within which all orders will likely be obeyed without question) is very large, authority rests on the hidden consent of the organization's members. Barnard quotes approvingly a passage conveying this point in reference to martial authority: "[an] inarticulate vote . . . is instantly taken by masses of men when the order comes to move forward . . . [T]he army does not move forward until the motion has 'carried.' " [25] While undoubtedly overdrawn, this passage contains a kernel of truth. Armies usually move forward even when the "motion" is "defeated," but they do so not in response to the authority of the general but out of fear of the "power" of the sergeants and lieutenants, who are instructed in most circumstances to deal harshly with anyone who refuses to advance. (It is said that the famous red coats worn by British infantrymen were intended to provide a better target for the sergeant's rifle should a soldier attempt to flee from battle.) Nevertheless, instances arise in every war where platoons or even large units in effect "mutiny" by disobeying the order to move forward. Whether such action evidences poor discipline on the part of the troops or faulty judgment by the commanding officers likely varies from situation to situation.

The "problem of coordination" involves on the one hand the difficulty of creating *uniformity* of action out of the diversity of individual purposes and interests; and on the other hand the necessity of offering attractive *incentives* to "persuade" individuals to sacrifice their private, personal goals to the goals of the organization. Uniformity is achieved by positing a coherent plan of action such that the separate activities of each subunit in the or-

25. *Ibid.*, p. 164.

ganization fit together to achieve common purposes.[26] Incentives are somewhat more complex. What will motivate individuals to contribute (time, effort, etc.) to an organization? Traditional theories about group behavior placed major emphasis on the role of common group interests as an incentive to support the organization. An individual will devote his energies to his trade union, his church organization, or his country's army because as a trade union member, churchgoer, or citizen he stands to benefit from the achievements of these groups in terms of better wages, a richer religious life, a more secure nation, etc. The flaw in this hypothesis was dramatically revealed by theorists like Mancur Olson who pointed out that *group* achievements constitute a form of "collective benefit"—available to members or organization *whether or not* they contribute to the organization's efforts. Why bother to be a loyal union man if you get the same wage regardless? Why fight in the army if you will be "defended" in any case? Counterarguments to the effect that each individual must contribute or the organization will collapse surely seem plausible only in the case of very small organizations or very high-ranking members of large organizations. The army example is worth pursuing. Not only does the civilian get defended even if he stays home, but (more to the point) in most wars he is far safer than the soldier who provides this "defense." Again *Catch-22* provides a perfect illustration. The "hero" Yossarian has gone to his su-

26.  This statement describes the "optimal" operation of an "ideal" organization. The actual operation of real organizations falls far short of this ideal. Subunits tend to develop a set of interests of their own which may be mutually incompatible. They therefore work at "cross-purposes" to one another, engaging in a process of politicking which can become quite conflictual. In view of such widespread "bureaucratic politics," discussion of the goals of the organization-as-a-whole seems inappropriate. (See in this regard the three models of decision-making outlined by Graham Allison in his seminal study *The Essence of Decision* (Boston: Little, Brown, 1971). But the general problem was anticipated by Rousseau, who carefully distinguished the "will of all" from the "general will" and cautioned against permitting corporate groups to influence the determination of the latter.)

perior officer to announce that he does not wish to fly any more combat missions. The Major tries several arguments to convince Yossarian that he "must" keep flying. Eventually he asks, "Would you like to see our country lose?" Yossarian replies matter-of-factly, "We can't lose. We've got more men, more money, and more material. There are ten million men in uniform who could replace me. . . . Let somebody else get killed." The Major responds with what he obviously believes to be a devastating rebuttal: "But suppose everybody on our side felt that way." Yossarian's answer turns the Major's hypothesis inside out: "Then I'd certainly be a damned fool to feel any other way. Wouldn't I?" [27]

How do organizations overcome the paradoxical weakness inherent in the "nonexcludable" nature of their collective benefits? One technique, instantly familiar, is to supplement the nonexcludable collective benefits with a variety of goods which can be given out selectively to those members who "pull their share." But the use of "selective incentives" is usually coupled with other techniques. John Kenneth Galbraith draws the central issues together in his discussion of "the motivating system."

Every organization postulates certain goals or purposes for the group as a whole, and these goals can act as very strong sources of motivation to accept authority within the organization. Galbraith introduces the terms "identification" and "adaptation" to characterize two important components of "the motivating system." By his definitions, *identification* is "the voluntary exchange of the individual's goals for the preferable ones of organization," while *adaptation* refers to "the association with organization in the hope of influencing its goals to accord more closely with the individual's own." Although Galbraith recognizes at least two other components of motivation (pecuniary incentives and coercion), identification and adaptation are the hallmarks of the modern economic system Galbraith calls "technostructure." In

27. Heller, *Catch-22*, p. 101.

his gloss on Karl Marx he contends that modernization and economic development have gradually eroded the importance of compulsion (which characterized the feudal era) and compensation (which replaced it under early capitalism). Especially in the "inner circle" of a modern organization, one discovers the motivational predominance of identification and adaptation, which indeed are closely interrelated:

> An individual, on becoming associated with an organization, will be more likely to adopt its goals in place of his own if he has hope of changing those he finds unsatisfactory or repugnant. And if he is strongly identified with the goals of an organization, he will be moved all the more strongly to try to improve it—to alter (i.e., adapt) any unsatisfactory goals so they accord with his own.[28]

## CONCLUSION

The institutionalization of authority aims at the smooth coordination of collective action. Yet even in the course of fulfilling this important function, authority can give rise to a large number of "disfunctions." Coexistent with the formally organized "lines of authority" one finds an extensive "network of influence" which some writers call the "informal organization." This term, according to Herbert Simon refers to "interpersonal relations in the organization that affect decisions within it but either are omitted from the formal scheme or are not consistent with that scheme." [29]

28. J. K. Galbraith, *The New Industrial State* (Boston: Houghton Mifflin, 1967), pp. 135–36. Notice that compensation and coercion are "power" motivators. A broader characterization would simply refer to positive and negative sanctions. Adaptation and identification, by contrast, operate independent of explicit sanctions, and from this perspective would constitute "influence" motivators. Thus the authority system as a whole features a synthesis of power, influence, and authority.
29. Simon, *Administrative Behavior*, p. 148. For a brilliant analysis of some of the pathological aspects of bureaucracies, see Robert Presthus, *The Organizational Society* (New York: Vintage Books, 1962).

The sales manager may be having an affair with the president's secretary; the comptroller and the vice-president may belong to the same exclusive country club. In short, informal relationships particularly among members of the organization who interact frequently on a face to face basis (usually using "influence" communication), may significantly outweigh the formal "paper" relationships, even to the point of effectively replacing them. Though authority nominally remains in the hands of the senior officer, it may have devolved for all practical purposes to one of his subordinates who consequently becomes the "real" boss. Moreover, certain people outside the lines of authority in formal positions of "influence" (i.e., advisers and other "staff" personnel) may similarly acquire control of the authority structure through the preponderant weight of their influence. A case in point is the fantastic extent of Henry Kissinger's influence over American foreign policy during the first five years of the Nixon era. Many outside observers came to regard Kissinger as second in authority only to Nixon himself despite his formal role as merely an (influence) adviser entirely outside the "line" positions held by the Secretary of State, Secretary of Defense, *et al.* In the fall of 1973 Kissinger's informal role was formalized: he assumed the position of Secretary of State.

# 3

# *Levels of Analysis: The Micro-Macro Problem*

The test of any concept's worth comes in its application to the analysis of "real" problems. The measure of worth is understanding: how well does a concept (or set of concepts) allow us to express an idea, describe a situation, evaluate the implications of action? What aspects of action are brought sharply into focus? What is obscured or overlooked?

In applying the concepts of power, influence, and authority we encounter immediately the problem of "units" and "levels" of analysis. Do we wish to use as the unit of analysis the individual or a plural unit such as a nation state? In one sense, there really is only one "unit" of analysis—the individual. All larger units are made up of individuals; all attempts to describe group action must come to grips with the fact that the group acts through and upon individual actors. To the extent that a group is "unified," the individuals within it have so coordinated their action (through power, influence, or most often authority) that they have succeeded in simulating the appearance of a single being free from "inner uncertainties." The term plural unit therefore implies concerted action by individuals who, properly coordinated, reach "group decisions" according to various procedures or rules of the game.

The problem of "levels of analysis" is much more challenging. Can we apply our concepts of power, influence, and authority to different levels of interaction? A useful distinction can be drawn between "micro" and "macro" analysis. To the economist micro refers to the actions of such relatively small units as companies[1] whose individual choices taken all together determine the macro-level activities of "the market." By analogy, micro in the present context denotes the viewpoint of the "individual looking up"; while the macro view examines the system of power, influence, and authority relations as a whole, "from the top looking down."

Most of the "grand theories" of politics describe power at the "macro" level—Plato's *Republic* envisions a society in which the authority of the guardians is unquestioned; Hobbes's *Leviathan* pictures a coordinated society literally within the body of the omnipotent sovereign; while Marx's harsh image portrays society as a "cold war" between the ruling bourgeoisie and the oppressed workers. While such theorists outline vividly their view of the broad patterns of macro relationships, they seldom devote much attention to the micro phenomena which these relationships comprise.

## POWER, INFLUENCE, AND AUTHORITY AT THE "MICRO" LEVEL

At the micro level, we are concerned to study the impact that power, influence, and authority have upon individuals. Let us assume that we can focus our attention on "deliberate action," excluding such involuntary activities as sleeping and breathing.

Our central axiom can thus be stated quite simply: "deliberate action" results from an internal process of decision-making in

1. Micro also refers to limited aspects of the total economic picture, such as supply and demand in the agricultural sector.

which the individual "makes up his mind" what to do. While this internal process cannot be observed we nevertheless hypothesize that it takes place. We further hypothesize that we can identify certain factors usually involved in this process and thus construct a "model" of what goes into the process of deciding what to do. This model is a summary rather than a reproduction—it concisely brings together some important features of decision-making but it does not necessarily tell us how they interact. The components include the following:

a)   an "objective situation"
b)   awareness of the situation (attention/perception)
c)   information about the situation (cognition/perception)
d)   memory (of other similar situations, etc.)
e)   language, or some other mechanism for structuring and comprehending "institutional facts"
f)   a set of ordered (?) preferences (value system)
g)   a set of alternative responses or strategies from which to choose
h)   a prediction (usually based at least in part on memory about the probable outcome of each strategy)
i)   a plan for action (or inaction)

The relationship among these components is illustrated in the diagram on page 73.

The bias of this model is clear enough: it reduces man to a "decision-maker" who "processes" information from the external environment, combines it with information stored "under his skin," and eventually arrives at a plan to "act" (or in the style of Hamlet, "not to act.") No one supposes that this model even vaguely approaches a complete model of human behavior—the only such model is man himself. Still it is peculiarly appropriate to the approach taken throughout this book to the phenomena of power, influence, and authority. For what we have been insisting all along is that these phenomena (usually) manifest themselves as *communications,* here defined as information "transmitted"

MODEL OF INDIVIDUAL'S DECISION-MAKING PROCESS

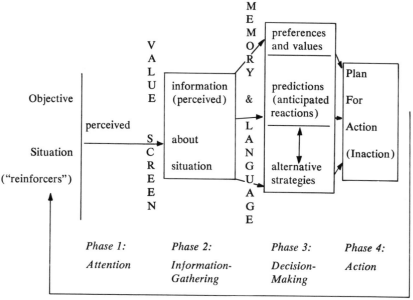

Phase 1: Attention

Phase 2: Information-Gathering

Phase 3: Decision-Making

Phase 4: Action

(feedback to the situation)

from another human being in the "external" environment. The question immediately arises: how do these three types of communication affect the decision-making process of the individual, and why?

Power communications appear the easiest to assimilate to the model. In its simplest form, a power communication purports to change the objective situation (positively or negatively) in "exchange" for a particular action or inaction. If you will do action X, I will do action Y which will either enhance or diminish your environment. The focus of power is, therefore, the external environment. To exercise power one must "control" a relevant aspect of that environment either directly (i.e., oneself) or indirectly (through other actors who for some reason will "do as they are told"). But the model reveals that the ostensibly objective emphasis of a power communication disguises a number of subjective implications usually just "taken for granted." For example, a power communication will not even enter into the individual's decision-making process if it is not noticed. The highwayman who yells out from his hiding place "Stop or I'll shoot" has for all intents and purposes zero impact on a passing traveler who is stone deaf. Thus a power communication must first be perceived. Moreover, it must be understood. The same injunction shouted in Chinese will be incomprehensible to a unilingual francophone. A Chinese speaker raised in a child's paradise of "robbers and good guys" where all guns are toys will seriously misinterpret the gravity of the situation. In all of these cases, however, the power communication can become effective if additional information is presented to or obtained by the "victim." The gunman may use gestures to convey his "meaning" to the deaf person, or indeed the Frenchman; he may take the time to explain to the grown-up child the distinction between toy and "real" guns. But even then his attempt to exert power may fail. The "victim" may remember a similar incident (perhaps with the same highwayman) in which the "threat" was not carried out.

Even lacking such memories the victims may "figure" that the gunman is bluffing and "predict" therefore that there is no need to comply. Or the victim may perceive that there are alternative strategies left out of the calculus presented by the gunman, and decide to flee, or to stay and "overpower" his assailant. Better still the victim may "calculate" that the alternative of stopping or getting shot for some reason does not constitute "an offer he can't refuse." The latter response is the basis for one of the late Jack Benny's famous comedy skits. Benny is walking home from the movies when a robber appears, brandishing a revolver, and demands, "Your money or your life!" A pause follows, which then becomes a prolonged silence. Stalling for more time, Benny shouts "I'm thinking it over."

It is always a mistake to explain a joke, but not so a lesson in human relations. The hilarity of the Benny skit only underscores the fundamental insight it contains: potential power-wielders assume that the "exchange" they offer is "worth it." In other words, they assume that their victim has a particular "preference ordering" or hierarchy of values such that the value they control (in this case life itself) is worth more than the value they demand from him in exchange (in this case money).

Finally, the victim may respond exactly as the gunman expected up to the point of formulating a plan for compliance, but then inadvertently fail to carry the plan through, perhaps falling down in what the gunman misconstrues as a threatening move. In short, at every stage in the process of decision-making, the individual may intentionally or unintentionally "disrupt" the effective operation of a power communication, thereby rendering it at the very least unsuccessful. The locus of power is external, "objective" to the individual, but compliance with power is a manifestly subjective phenomenon. So too is noncompliance.

While power tends to ignore the subjective aspects of decision-making—assuming that manipulation of the objective situation will lead to compliance—influence reverses this emphasis. The defining characteristic of an influence communication is that it leaves the objective situation as it is, focusing instead on the internal components of decision-making. Again we may work through the model to show the several facets of influence. At the risk of tedious repetition, most of the problems raised in the "power" examples could simply be reinterpreted as instances of influence if we postulate the intervention of a third party "adviser" to the victim.[2] "Look out—there's a gunman behind those bushes" (attention) or "that's a *real* gun he's holding" (cognition). In both of these examples, *additional information* affects the early phase of decision-making. But similar interventions can also affect other phases: "Remember last week when this guy tried to hold

---

2.  Notice that some of these influence communications could be delivered by the gunman himself. In the earlier set of examples, his "explanation" about the distinction between toy and real guns provides an illustration.

you up?" or "He's telling you to hand over your money." The opportunities for influence touch every component of decision-making: "Why don't you try to get away?" (a "new strategy" is identified); "If you move, he'll shoot." (prediction); "I know money is important to you, Jack, but is it worth risking your life?" (preference).

In each case of influence, the objective situation remains undisturbed. Instead, the perception of that situation, or some other component of decision-making, is altered with a view to changing the outcome (i.e., the phase of "final decision"). Viewed from this perspective, influence appears at once to be more pervasive and potentially more precise than power. Its bases are not *control* of the environment but *knowledge* about the environment and an insight into the decision-making process by which individuals choose how to act in their environment.

At this point we may be tempted to "correct" Bacon's famous aphorism: knowledge is influence, not power. In fact, however, knowledge can be used in either way. Superior knowledge may permit an individual to play an "influence role" as adviser; used differently, it creates a "power role" as a wholesaler or retailer of knowledge. The former relationship treats knowledge as a background resource for an interpersonal exchange; the latter relationship makes knowledge the currency of exchange itself.[3]

Despite the important operational differences just noted between power communications and influence communications, both share one essential feature in common: each type of communication presents the individual with a *choice* to be made as a result of what we have called the decision-making process. Authority, by contrast, goes much further, denying the very possibility, or more accurately, the necessity of choice. For in its pure form, an

3. Thus Lasswell and Kaplan include "enlightenment" as one of their eight basic values. The others are power (!!), respect, rectitude, affection, well-being, wealth, and skill. See Harold Lasswell and Abraham Kaplan, *Power and Society* (New Haven: Yale University Press, 1970).

authority communication omits all reference whatsoever to either consequences or alternatives. Instead it presents for immediate adoption an already formulated "plan for action." The process of decision-making itself is abrogated. To accept authority is to make a policy decision to forgo future weighing of alternatives or calculation of costs and benefits. From this perspective, the brilliant definition earlier quoted from Herbert Simon gains new significance: Simon tells us that in placing himself "under the authority" of another, an individual *"sets himself a general rule which permits the communicated decision of another to guide his own choice* (i.e., to serve as a premise of those choices) without deliberation on his own part on the expediency of those premises." (Emphasis in original.)

To accept authority, therefore, is to place one's own decision-making process (perhaps only temporarily, perhaps only with respect to certain types of decisions) in the hands of someone else. In terms of the model outlined above, the input of an authoritative communication "short circuits" the decision-making process, skipping through all of the phases to become immediately and directly the "plan" for action itself.

If this interpretation of authority is correct, how could one possibly justify or even rationalize the existence of authority? Surely, authority at the very least subverts irremediably any possible claim to individual autonomy. Surely it replaces "man the decision-maker" with an even lower humanoid species, "man the non-decision-maker" or "man the automaton." [4] Before we rush headlong into the camp of the anarchists (who would probably only smile and say, "This is what we have been telling you all along"), it should be remembered that one basis for the non-decision-making that characterizes acceptance of authority may be a *prior* decision based on considerations related to either power

4.  Note that the use of the term *nondecision* in this context differs from the interpretation intended by Peter Bachrach and Morton Baratz in their famous articles, revised and published in their book *Power and Poverty* (New York: Oxford University Press, 1970).

or influence. In other words, an individual may have been persuaded or otherwise induced to accept authority in order to obvi-
ate the need for ponderous choices in later situations.[5] This observation suggests criteria by which we might determine whether
the prior decision is "rational" or "economical." Do we gain
more (e.g., in "opportunity benefits") through avoiding later decision-making than we lose through agreeing in advance to do
things which could turn out to be distasteful or contrary to our
values?[6] But the hoary problem of "rationality" need not detain
us here. The important point is that rationally or irrationally,
for various reasons most individuals do indeed find it useful, ex-
pedient, or necessary to "accept authority." And yet we should
be careful not to assume that all authority originates in conscious,
deliberate decisions "not to decide." (The point recalls the delightful comment by the Admiral in *HMS Pinafore,* who proudly
recollects that as a Member of Parliament "I always voted at my
party's call, and I never thought of thinking for myself at all.")

From a different perspective, authority communications are
successful when the individual has *internalized values or norms
favoring obedience* to such communications from a particular
source on a particular range of subject matters. The usefulness of

5.  This justification for authority parallels Robert Dahl's "criterion of
    economy." See Dahl, *After the Revolution?,* p. 8 and *passim.*
6.  James Coleman ("Loss of Power," *American Sociological Review,*
    XXXVIII, 1, 1973, p. 3) throws a different light on the mystery of au-
    thority by showing that the loss of freedom involved in joining a
    corporate body (i.e., accepting its authority) is presumably compen-
    sated by an increase in power through access to combined resources
    and other collective benefits: "When a person decides to yield control
    of his resources to a corporate body (e.g., to pay union dues or to
    obey union strike calls), he expects to gain the greater power of com-
    bined resources. The decision is between acting independently with
    more freedom or collectively with more power."

    Note, however, that Mancur Olson's critique of the "logic of
    collective action" seriously questions the appeal of such reasoning,
    since by their very nature collective benefits are available regardless
    of whether one pays the costs.

this interpretation is that it permits us to examine the discussion in Chapter 2 of learning obedience. The "socialization process," with all its connotations of invisibility and pre- or non-rationality, largely determines both the presence of the value of obedience and its place in the normative hierarchy. Whether one views learning in terms of "power-conditioning" (i.e., the manipulation of the contingencies of reinforcement) or in terms of "influence-insight" (i.e., the guidance of perceptions through example, advice, etc.)[7] the results are similar: authority is able to function because children continue to learn the value of obedience, often at a relatively young age. But unless obedience is learned as the "highest value," we can predict that an authority communication will "fail" if it threatens or otherwise impinges upon another value which occupies a higher place on the hierarchy. Very few individuals would accept an order to commit suicide. Even the Kamikaze missions flown in World War II by Japanese pilots (whose sense of obedience was legendary) were "voluntary." Even Hobbes, an authoritarian *par excellence,* permitted the citizen whose life was in jeopardy to resist the authority of the Leviathan. In general, individuals who never learn obedience, or who internalize it at a relatively low position in their value hierarchy, will prove "resistant" to authority. Ironically, in this category one finds both saints and criminals.

Insofar as the acceptance of authority abrogates the element of choice that defines moral action,[8] the exercise of authority

---

7.  Cf. William Eckhardt, *Compassion,* p. 133: ". . . the Behaviorist theory of learning would be a power theory of learning, while the Gestalt theory of learning would be an influence theory of learning."
8.  I am not suggesting that acceptance of authority excuses one from giving a moral account of one's actions. On the contrary, the decision to accept authority must be subjected to continuous critical evaluation and re-evaluation. We have only ourselves to blame if we become seduced into mindless, unquestioning obedience. A central goal of the teaching of political ethics is to raise to consciousness the implications of accepting authority.

carries with it an enormous burden of responsibility.[9] It turns the "subject" into a kind of automaton, a mere extension of the strength of the "authority figure" himself. Precisely for this reason, of course, authority unifies collective action in a spectacularly successful manner. No one recognized this more clearly than Hobbes himself, who wrote in Chapter 10 of *Leviathan*: "The greatest of human powers, is that which is compounded of the powers of most men, united by consent, in one person, natural, or civil, that has the use of all their powers depending on his will; such as is the power of a commonwealth. . . ." The mechanism for attaining such "strengths united" is what we have been describing as authority backed by power; the result is Leviathan, pictured on the frontispiece of the 1651 edition as a huge "artificial person" whose very body is composed of the united bodies of the individuals who are his "subjects." Yet, especially after Nuremburg, we have rejected the defense so common among functionaries in every setting that "I was only following orders." Or have we? Obedience to manifestly illegal and even unconstitutional orders appeared repeatedly among officials in President Nixon's administration, who, it would seem, merely wanted assurance that these orders came from "very high up." (At times it is difficult to tell whether they were referring to the President or to some higher deity.)

Since an authority communication attempts to "short circuit" the individual's decision-making process, we must be concerned with whether the exercise of authority is self-perpetuating or self-terminating. Self-perpetuating authorities emphasize discipline and the perfection of automatic obedience. Self-terminating authorities appreciate the temporary loss of autonomy involved in sub-

9. In recognition of this dilemma, Max Weber formulated his famous notion of the "ethic of responsibility" as a guide to the moral problems peculiar to leaders who must exercise authority. See his "Politics as a Vocation." The other side of this particular coin is the need for "trust" in those who exercise authority. When trust is shaken, authority is automatically undermined.

mitting to authority, and thus they strive to heighten the awareness and critical faculties of the (temporary) subject and to
transfer to him whatever knowledge or skills are necessary to permit
him at some later stage "to make decisions for himself." Marx's
"utopian" vision of a society without government represents an
extrapolation of the hypothesis that all authority can and should
"self-destruct" after it has served its purpose.

## POWER, INFLUENCE, AND AUTHORITY AT THE MACRO LEVEL

Up to this point our discussion has focused on the individual,
particularly the question of how power, influence, and authority
affect individual decision-making. While understanding the micro
level is essential, it is necessary also to make some observations
about the macro implications of these concepts. The central macro
question is: *how are power, influence and authority distributed in
the system as a whole?*

The macro-level question obviously touches on the debate
that raged through social science circles in the 1960's over the
"proper" way to measure the distribution of power in American
society.[10]

10. Actually, the measurement issue has had both micro and macro implications. While at the macro level measurement of *distribution* was
foremost, at the micro level, researchers tried to measure *"amount"*
of power. Most scholars defined amount of power in terms of the
difference between expected behavior (in the absence of the exercise
of power), and behavior resulting from the intervention of the power-
wielder. Leaving aside the conceptual and methodological difficulties
of trying to quantify and estimate behavior observed and behavior
assumed to have otherwise occurred, it seems to me ultimately impossible to determine whether power, influence, or authority has
worked until we develop a complete theory of motivation and are
able to obtain perfect knowledge about "subjects." As much insight
can be gained through speculative indwelling in the minds of political
participants as through attempts at quantification or experimental
analysis. The thrust of the present critique of measurement is therefore to deflate the balloon of oversimplified assumptions and to re-

Our approach would suggest that adequate treatment of the "problem of distribution" entails a *threefold* task of "measuring" not only the distribution of power in society but also the distribution of influence and authority. The remarks that follow represent a critique of the approach to this problem rather than a substantive effort to present the relevant "facts." It may be useful to reiterate here our earlier contention that most scholars have worried about measuring power when they should have taken more time trying to *conceptualize* it more satisfactorily, i.e., so as to take account of influence and authority as well. With this comment clearly in mind, we may begin our macro analysis. Perhaps the reader will find it helpful to imagine that he or she is magically able "to look down on society from above," and observe the vast network of power, influence, and authority relationships. This is the "macro perspective"; the task is to discern the pattern of these relationships.

## Power

Power implies the existence of a valued object[11] that a) can be manipulated (i.e., increased or diminished by one actor with respect to another); b) is valued by the respondent; c) is in rela-

---

direct attention to the perhaps insurmountable task of conceptual analysis, at the same time alerting students of politics to the complex array of possible factors in interpersonal relationships that entail power, influence, or authority.

11.    It is essential to emphasize the dual connotation of the term "value." In one sense, values are *objects* "out there" which people find "valuable." In a quite different sense values are *subjective dispositions* toward things out there, or in other words the value attached to objects. Manipulation of valued objects is the essence of power; manipulation of subjective values is an aspect of influence. Ability to do the former does not necessarily entail ability to do the latter, and vice versa.

Game theorists use the term "utility" to bring together the subjective and objective connotations of value. An actor's decision can be altered either by changing the "objective" character of the relevant "payoff matrix" or by affecting some aspect of his perception of that matrix. See the discussion of game theory in the conclusion below.

tively short supply; and d) is "divisible." Any object fulfilling these criteria can become the basis of a power relationship.

Physical well-being and money provide obvious examples, but there are other less obvious ones as well: consider the role of liquor during prohibition or the manipulation of affection in a love affair. Harold Lasswell and Abraham Kaplan have prepared an "inventory" of eight basic values that underly various types of social exchange. Besides well-being, wealth, and affection, the list includes skill, enlightenment, respect, rectitude, and "power" it- self. (In this context power appears to mean office or authority.) These eight values are used to develop an elaborate typology of sixty-four "forms of influence and power" ranging from "com- pulsion" to "censorship," from "advertising" to "zeal." [12] Who- ever controls valued objects has the potential to exercise power. But while values constitute the bases for power relationships, language provides the medium for power exchanges. The exercise of power is literally couched in statements *about* values. If this observation gives the impression that people are always talking about values rather than manipulating them, at least it may correct the overemphasis in the opposite direction. Ultimately of course values must at least occasionally be manipulated as "proof" of the credibility of threats and promises. But social exchanges re- semble bookkeeping practices insofar as "paper" symbols (en- tries, dollar bills, etc.) are accepted "at face value." In addition to studying the distribution of primary values, therefore, one must

---

12. The typology consists of a matrix of the eight values conceived as both the "base" for the exchange (base value) and the "scope" or object of the exchange (scope value). The valued object becomes the base for a power relationship in which A "offers" (threatens or promises) to increase or diminish B's share of value $V_1$ in exchange for B's performance of action X or B's reciprocation with $V_2$. (In the terminology of Lasswell and Kaplan, $V_1$ is the "base" value, $V_2$ the "scope" value.) Despite the suggestiveness of the typology, Lass- well and Kaplan's discussion in general is paralyzed by their tendency to use the same words (especially power and influence) in half a dozen or more distinct senses. *Power and Society,* p. 87 and *passim.*

look as well at the distribution of credibility. He who is *believed* to control important values may be able to use successfully threats and promises based on those values. (It is in this indirect, almost accidental, way that those power-measurers who use the "reputational" method may have stumbled onto something significant.)

One condition for the equal distribution of power would appear to be the equal distribution of the *resources of power*—the valued objects that can serve as the basis of a power relationship. But more is involved. Since power is expressed in communications which must be believed to be effective, the *distribution of credibility* is also relevant.[13] Of equal importance is the *nature of the communications system* itself. Who has *access* to communication? In a dyadic relationship we may distinguish symmetrical from asymmetrical communication structures: if A can talk to B, can B talk back? Who gets to talk first? Who gets the "last word?" These simple but fundamental questions take on vast complexity in a large social setting, further complicating the task of measuring the "distribution of power."

### Influence

At the systems level influence appears to be far less stable than power. Who influences whom? In a sense we all influence each other. Every time we have a conversation with someone (not necessarily a power talk or an authority exchange) we are probably influenced by what we see and hear, touch, feel, and smell. How could such a vast web of influence ever be measured, much less recognized? One would need a thorough inventory of the entire network of social relationships which would then be evaluated both quantitatively in terms of their frequency and qualitatively in terms of their intensity and emotional content. We might also want to "scale" these relationships along a continuum

13.   Cf. Hobbes's discussion of "reputation" as an "instrumental power" and his general argument that much power rests on opinion. (*Leviathan*, ch. 10.)

that ranges from "intimate" to "frozen." [14] Having thus established a snapshot picture of the social valences, one might then produce a film of the shifts in the valence structure and in the behavior of the participants. But unless the moving picture covered an enormous stretch of time we would miss entirely the impact of early influences like the socialization process as determinants of the social relationships of the present and future. Moreover, our entire approach would limit us to overt goings-on. Entirely eclipsed from view would be the invisible but equally important covert activities (associated with "tacit influence") occurring inside the heads of all our "subjects." To study the distribution of influence is to study the whole concept of society, especially the subjective sense of society which permits "socialized interactants" to live, work, and play together.

Recognizing the impossibility of a complete study of the distribution of influence, we might lower our sights to study aspects of influence in a fairly well-defined setting such as a segment of a bureaucracy. Here we would undoubtedly find people in "influence roles" as advisers, planners, and other "staff" personnel. But beneath the surface of these relationships are profoundly important factors often conveyed better by novelists than political scientists. (If this discussion accomplishes nothing more than to encourage modesty among professional students of the "political process" it will in my view have served its purpose.)

### Authority

In organizational settings, authority implies hierarchy insofar as those "further up" make decisions for, or otherwise direct the

14. Scott and Lyman differentiate talk into "linguistic styles . . . ordered on a scale of decreasing social intimacy." They call these the *intimate, casual, consultative, formal,* and *frozen* styles. While conceivably power, influence, and authority could be expressed in any style, *normally* one finds influence dominant in the first three, authority in the fourth, and power in the fifth. Stanford Lyman and Marvin B. Scott, "Accounts," *American Sociological Review,* XXXIII, 1 (1968), pp. 55ff.

actions of, their subordinates. If A has authority over B in regard to X, B cannot also have authority over A in regard to X. Similarly, if in regard to X, A has authority over B and B over C, then C cannot have authority over A. Nevertheless, it is possible for a subordinate in one authority setting or issue area to enjoy the role of superior in a different setting: the traffic cop may give "orders" to the commissioner of police.

By definition, those near the top of organizational hierarchies have therefore "more authority" than those beneath them. But we must not forget our earlier distinctions between formal and informal authority structures, or the crucial point that the distribution of influence and power *may not* be congruent with the distribution of authority. The net result could conceivably be a fairly egalitarian distribution of the total resources and the capabilities of control.

Although authority is obviously distributed unevenly according to position in a hierarchy (those "higher up" have more of it), there are several additional ways in which authority can be divided. First, authority may be apportioned to different institutions having jurisdiction over specific issue areas. Thus, for example, the United States Congress alone has the authority to declare war, but the President has sole authority to act as commander in chief of the armed forces. (Numerous Presidents have used this authority to fight undeclared wars.) Second, authority may be parceled out to different units of government on a regional or territorial basis.

The first device is called "separation of powers"; the second is best exemplified in "federalism." (Arthur Maass and his associates introduced the terms capital division of powers (cdp) and areal division of powers (adp) to make this same distinction.) Both arrangements usually require elaborate written and/or unwritten constitutional provisions which may necessitate a further division of authority: the institution of a judiciary to interpret disputes arising from the constitutional division of authority.

A third technique for distributing authority is to "delegate" it to a person or group further down or even entirely outside the authority structure. An element of constitutionalism inevitably surrounds delegated authority as well because of the need to specify "terms of reference" to determine the limits of permissible "discretion" (how much authority is being given for what purposes?) and to ensure means for evaluating subsequent exercises of authority. When terms of reference are vague, discretion is broad, and oversight inadequate, the person or agency to whom authority is delegated can become almost entirely autonomous and "irresponsible." Thus delegated authority often resembles divided authority, despite the provisions (at least in theory) to ensure strict accountability and a coherent set of responsibilities and duties.

Even in the most authoritarian societies, the facts of size and complexity militate against the establishment of a single coherent hierarchy of governmental authority for the entire nation. Instead authority is fragmented through areal and capital division and through the tendency toward autonomy of agencies, commissions, and bureaucratic units to whom supposedly limited authority has been delegated. Thus one looks in vain for a single "authority structure" in advanced industrial society, finding instead myriad competing authority structures engaged in a complicated process of politicking amongst themselves involving power and influence far more frequently than the mere exercise of authority. In most instances, authority works the way the textbooks describe it in small-scale entities rather than larger systems. To be sure, a few authoritative decisions take effect on a large system such as a nation-state. But local agencies do not simply follow orders handed down from higher authorities. Commissions are not passive instruments which implement a master plan formulated by national (legislative) authorities.

If authority at the level of the nation-state is fragmented in terms of its formal structure, is it nevertheless unified in purpose? A naïve response might postulate some notion of the "public good" as the touchstone for the exercise of all authority. From this perspective, fragmentation might appear inconsequential, a matter of accessibility and administrative convenience. On the contrary, however, decentralized authority does not replicate national authority at a lower level, despite the often striking architectural similarities that are evidence of a strong predisposition to imitate and reproduce at least the physical setting for authoritative decision-making. Notwithstanding the insistence by Yves Simon that "the common good is central to every theory of authority. It is only in relation to it that authority exercises the central functions . . . ," [15] the truth of the matter is that the very notion of the public good itself has become problematical.

Indeed, so powerful have modern corporations become that economists like John Kenneth Galbraith have reversed classical economic assumptions about "consumer sovereignty" in favor of a "revised sequence" in which large corporations shape demand, fix prices, and plan production so as to "subsume the market." So-called public goods such as security and defense are defined largely in terms of the private interests of large corporations, which seek to legitimize their appeal for government funding and support under the generous cloak of the "public good." Supposedly designed to produce a collective benefit to every American citizen, defense spending in the United States is closely tied in to the deeply vested interests of the military establishment and the industrial corporations whose continued existence depends on large defense contracts. Corporate lobbying and politicking determine in large part expenditures from the public purse across a vast range of defense spending, which accounts for a large portion of every dollar paid out by the United States government.

Despite widespread criticism of the slogan "What's good for General Motors is good for the country," there nevertheless seems to be more agreement about what's good for General Motors than there is about what's good for the country. In the absence of a consensus on the proper functions and purposes of governmental authority, authoritative decision-making will continue to respond

15.  Yves Simon, *A General Theory of Authority* (Notre Dame, Ind.: University of Notre Dame Press, 1962), p. 157.

more readily to the demands of pressure groups than to the needs of society.

Given the almost chaotic fragmentation of authority, is coherence among decision-makers somehow obtained through power and influence? A version of this hypothesis has given rise to the theory of the "power elite" associated with such radical sociologists as C. Wright Mills. But the term itself is ambiguous: does the power elite comprise the authority elite and the influence elite? Only after we have answered this very fundamental question can we evaluate the central hypotheses of elite theory, and resolve the conflict between the elitists who claim that there is considerable coordination, and the pluralists who deny that it exists.[16]

Having examined aspects of the distribution of authority, let us turn our attention briefly to the means of its exercise. How is it possible from a technical standpoint to set up a system of authoritative communication that extends over vast areas or that survives countless changes of generations? Viewed from this perspective, authority can be seen to be based not on a mopopoly of coercion (as Weber insisted) but on a monopoly over the system of communications and/or transportation. Indeed, the particular type of communications system will affect whether authority is "space binding" or "time binding." In the former case, authority spreads over a large area but may last a relatively short time; in the latter, authority is limited in areal extent but it persists over a long period of time.

16. The whole debate was moved to a much higher level, at least temporarily, by Bachrach and Baratz who pointed out that the overt behavior studied by both schools may be less important than the behavior that is excluded (i.e., nonbehavior) because elites and perhaps masses as well hold certain values that a priori exclude even from consideration a number of possible courses of action. In their terminology, the fact that for years women automatically accepted a position of relative inferiority toward men can be viewed as a "nondecision" by women regarding their own status. One function of so-called "liberation movements" is to raise to consciousness courses of action previously excluded from consideration as a result of such nondecisions.

Certain types of media (e.g., parchment, clay, and stone) emphasize time because they are so durable in nature. Media such as papyrus and paper are less durable but much lighter in weight and are therefore "suited to wide areas in administration and trade." Empires (space binding) rely on written communication that permits laws and decrees of a uniform nature to be communicated to the outlying areas of the empire, and reports and other feedbacks to be reliably relayed to the center of the empire. In the time-binding village or tribe, authority takes the form of traditions and customs preserved from the ancient past, and handed on to succeeding generations. In short, different types of communication systems have different types of "bias" toward either centralization or decentralization. A revolution in communications is capable of disrupting and even transforming the distribution of authority.[17]

17.    For extensions of these ideas see the numerous published writings of Canadian economist Harold Adams Innis.

# 4

## Conclusion:
## Concepts and Action

We have spent considerable time examining three concepts with an implicit expectation that the exercise is worthwhile. Now let us consider some further practical implications of this conceptual analysis. The wider context of this consideration involves the general relationship between concepts and action, and this remains an issue of heated controversy amongst students of politics. Indeed, the issue entails the relationship between theory and practice, or thought and action. Marx formulated the notion of *praxis* as a kind of synthesis, illustrated by the maxim: "Act like a man of thought; think like a man of action." T. S. Eliot, in "Choruses from the Rock," struck a similar theme, referring to "The endless cycle of idea and action."

Must every action be preceded by an explicit thought-concept? No clear-cut answer has been given. Nevertheless, it does seem that a given conceptual scheme can obscure the action alternatives perceived by a potential actor, especially by posing pseudo-choices based on simplified dichotomies. For example, if we do not possess an adequate concept of influence, we may be blind to its possible uses in "real" situations. Hannah Arendt's dis-

cussion of the concepts of "power" and "violence" provides a case
in point. In an attempt to explore much of the same "conceptual
space" with which we have been concerned, Arendt distinguishes
between power and violence in the following manner:

> *Power* corresponds to the human ability not just to act, but
> to act in concert. Power is never the property of an individual;
> it belongs to a group and remains in existence only so long as
> the group keeps together.

> Power springs up whenever people get together and act in
> concert.

> *Violence* . . . is close to strength since the implements of
> violence . . . are designed and used for the purpose of
> multiplying natural strength. . . .[1]

In Arendt's terms, power is an attribute not of the individual
(who can be said only to possess "strength"), but of the tightly
coordinated group capable of acting in concert. Violence by contrast may be used by the lone individual desperately trying to
"subdue" a group through the artificially inflated strength which
the implements of violence have made possible. Picture a man with
a machine gun holding a group of legislators at bay. This exemplifies the contrast between violence and power in Arendtian terms.
Surely, however, the potential for action exceeds the narrowly
circumscribed polar possibilities Arendt seems to envision. Arendt
herself insists that terms like influence and authority be defined
separately, and yet she concentrates all her analysis on power and
violence. Some might argue in Arendt's defense that she has identified the polar extremities of action leaving to more mundane
students the task of "filling in" the intervening conceptual space
with concepts like influence. If this is so, Arendt has never elaborated this interpretation. Moreover, in one of her essays she at-

1.  Hannah Arendt, *On Violence,* pp. 44, 46, 52.

tempts to remove from discussion the concept of authority on the grounds that it "has disappeared from the modern world."

The image Arendt conveys of power as pure coordinated action (one is tempted to say, "perfect authority") contrasts sharply with the "conflict theorists'" notion of power as often ruthless suppression, the iron fist in the velvet glove, or as one writer has defined it, "the capacity to harm." Where Arendt sees cooperation in pursuit of collective goals, theorists like C. Wright Mills see conflict and the antagonism of interests.

Undoubtedly both are at least partially correct, and yet neither theorist's concepts can comprehend the other's world. In terms of political action, the practical implication of Mills's theory is violence to overcome exploitation; of Arendt's, negotiation and debate to reach decision. Each presents us with a *single* lens through which to view the socio-political world. Given our astigmatism and myopia, we probably need more than one lens. Yet merely to "pick up" different theoretical lenses, one after another, ultimately leads to vertigo. We must somehow look through several compatible lenses at the same time.[2] "Power," "influence," and "authority" help us "see" politics more clearly.


STUDYING POLITICS AS COMMUNICATION

If politics is communication, we must study who talks to whom and what they say. Even a complete analysis of "who talks to whom," however, would fail to yield a "complete" picture of

2. Anyone disturbed by the prospect of simultaneously peering through three conceptual lenses should consult the text of Jean Laponce's presidential address to the Canadian Political Science Association, "Of Gods, Devils, Monsters, and One-Eyed Variables." *Canadian Journal of Political Science* VII, 2, June 1974. Laponce suggests that students of politics should somehow develop three "eyes," one for positive attributes of a political problem, the second for negative attributes, and the third for neutral attributes. Apparently I am not the only political scientist who has a rather bizarre imagination.

power, influence, and authority. Power and influence are often "communicated" in a nonverbal and sometimes unconscious manner. People can be "influenced" by the "example" of someone who is totally oblivious to the existence of the relationship. Similarly, someone can "exert" power simply by displaying or shifting the resources of power even without "exercising" power through the issuance of a power communication.

The advice that we begin our study of power, influence, and authority with an analysis of "political talk" does not intend to suggest that we end there as well, even if it does discourage the belief that complete understanding is possible. A useful first step is to examine patterns of communication in an attempt to locate and describe the "nerves of government." But we must not allow ourselves to be seduced by the slick assertion that the medium is the message. The medium is after all merely the medium. We must look not only at the form but also at the content of communication. What is said and how?

The study of content can never be reduced to structure, i.e., the formal characteristics of communications in terms, for example, of the paradigms outlined in Chapter 1. Our concern must be *interpretive* as well as analytic. Structural or quantitative linguistic analysis is only a prelude to understanding the "meaning" of communication to *both* the "sender" *and* the "receiver." (Their perceptions may not be congruent. My attempt to "influence" you may seem through your eyes a "power" move.) It is imperative, therefore, to study the socio-political context of a particular communication as well as the verbal expression itself, and to synthesize both by exploring the meaning given the communication by the interactors.

Perhaps the most effective way to illustrate the importance of context is to consider the problem of studying power, influence, and authority in highly repressive societies. In particular, the sense of severe limitations on political discourse (i.e., public speech) conditions the politics of such societies. One must be very careful what one "says" outside—and even in some cases inside—the "privacy" of the home; public discourse must follow closely the "party line"; unorthodox speech carries high costs. Even the sciences are subject to linguistic supervision. As for the arts, censorship is nearly always severe. Political humor critical of the regime is about as welcome as religious heresy was in medieval Europe.

The emphasis on "correct" speech carries paradoxical implications. So overpowering is its effect that the populace may become mute and apathetic. People "have no opinions" about public issues—to speak at all is to risk committing heresy. A *New York Times* article on Iran nicely illustrates the point; it is worth quoting at length:

> Savak [the Iranian secret police] is reliably said to permeate all levels of Iranian life and to keep close surveillance on those considered potential dissidents. For these reasons, Iranian intellectuals, students, businessmen, and Government officials rarely discuss possible misgivings about the Shah with anyone but their most trusted friends, and virtually never with foreigners. . . . An Iranian government official, politely telling a foreigner that Iranian government officials do not criticize the Shah and his work, said with a smile, "I am sure there are many other things we can talk about. Perhaps carpets." [3]

In such societies, disagreement with policy (if it exists at all) tends to be registered not in speech but in *action*—lack of productivity, pilfering, and other forms of petty sabotage may become commonplace. Quotas cannot be met because "physical conditions" stand in the way. Since refusal or noncooperation on personal grounds is illegitimate ("I don't *want* to do extra work," or "I've done *my* share," or "I've got *better* things to do"), workers seek refuge in mendacious excuses: "I can't work Sunday because my wife is sick."

If the strategies of "resistance" take on a kind of deviousness, in which public enthusiasm for the official pronouncements dis-

---

3.  James F. Clarity, "Rich but Underdeveloped, Iran Seeks More Power," *New York Times*, June 3, 1974, p. 12.

guises private disagreement manifested in noncooperation, strategies of "control" are distinctive in a different way. Leaders manipulate the official ideology in influence language designed to generate participation and support. Explicit use of authority or power language is frowned upon. Occasionally, however, specific regions or individuals are "singled out" for extensive power attention either in the form of lavish praise and reward or devastating criticism and punishment. Thus through concentrated but economical marshaling of power resources (followed by widespead publicity), a not too subtle influence message is conveyed: if you want praise (or to avoid blame) you should act (or avoid acting) in such and such a manner. One strength of this form of indirect influence communication is that people draw their own conclusions—they are "shown" what they "should" do instead of being "told" what they "have" to do. Explicit instructions, by contrast, have two liabilities:

a)   they outline by implication what people do *not* have to do

b)   they apply only to those to whom they are specifically sent, thereby relieving nonrecipients of the responsibility of compliance.

While virtually all large-scale organizations face analogous problems which they confront using roughly similar strategies of control, certain regimes appear to have developed these practices to a very sophisticated art. To study such societies without examining the political culture within which power, influence, and authority operate and trying to decode the "hidden messages" that condition political behavior would be to overlook crucial (if invisible) aspects of their "political reality." [4]

This advice may appear to favor "traditional" political science methods over newer "quantitative" techniques. Labels aside, we badly need to place political science squarely within the ambit

---

4.   I am indebted to my colleague Professor Grey Hodnett for suggesting some of these applications to me.

of other "interpretive sciences" by developing a special branch of "hermeneutics" related to political relations. Given the richness and vastness of the subject, the ideas expressed in this book amount to only an introduction to far more sophisticated study of communication as the medium of power, influence, and authority.

The focus of such studies remains, however, the way in which interactors communicate with one another. Our concern with "word politics" can be pursued in settings as diverse as marital arguments and international conflict. Stanley Hoffmann pointed in this direction when he wrote:

> The distinction between acts and verbal policies is losing its usefulness. It used to be true that great powers could act, whereas the smaller ones could mainly talk. Now, when the most spectacular kind of action—military action—is either very much under controls or displayed primarily for purposes of denial, when the smaller states can act quite effectively either through subversion or diplomatic bargaining, when threats are more frequent and productive than "real" moves and more evenly distributed, the distinction no longer makes much sense. It is rather futile to ask as a criterion of "seriousness," how many divisions the Pope has at a time when the Emperor can hardly use his divisions or must sink them into a morass opened by guerrillas. For the ratio of purely verbal policies is extraordinarily high today in everyone's foreign policy. The discord between the super-powers, which prevents a final showdown and final settlements, condemns each to a policy of proclamations and declamations for the record. The universal competition for prestige (which can be lost through excess use of force) and the prevalence of wielding influence and using mild forms of coercion put a premium on verbalism. The importance of signals, messages, communications in bargaining situations like today's (marked by mixed interests and limited force) implies that verbal policies are indeed policies and tantamount to acts insofar as they affect an opponent's understanding of a nation's attitude and reactions. What is deterrence if not a nexus of credible threats, i.e. of verbal policies? . . . To a large extent, verbal policies are a substitute for acts that would lead to doomsday, just as the proliferation

of strategic theorizing in peacetime is a substitute for strategic
action that would lead to the holocaust. In both instances, the
substitutes communicate more than a state of mind; they indicate a state of will.[5]

Word politics has come to dominate world politics and to
eclipse non-verbal politics. Words are the instruments of power,
influence, and especially authority. Thus words themselves have
political significance. Hobbes's *Leviathan* was, among other things,
the "sovereign definer," exercising absolute authority over the
meaning of terms and the publication of doctrines. But no one
appreciated the political significance of words more than George
Orwell, whose brilliant satire on "Newspeak" (written three dec-
ades ago) today appears uncannily prophetic. To control thought
(and therefore action) effectively, one must control language and
meaning. The "inner party" in 1984 jealously guards the uses of
language and resorts to such practices as the rewriting of history
and the redefinition of words and phrases. After thorough indoctrination, the inhabitants of Oceania could accept without question that "freedom is slavery" and that "two and two make five."
Instrumental in this learning process was the vocabulary imposed
on them by the Inner Party, respectfully called "Newspeak." The
vocabulary of Newspeak was divided into three groups. The A
vocabulary consisted of words "needed for the business of everyday life—for such things as eating, drinking, working, putting on
one's clothes, going up and down stairs. . . ." [6] Although some
of these words were similar to the ones used today in ordinary
English, they had become few in number and rigid in meaning,
purged of all ambiguity. The result was intentional: "it would
have been quite impossible to use the A vocabulary for literary

5.  Stanley• Hoffmann, *Gulliver's Troubles* (New York: McGraw-Hill,
    1968), pp. 63–64.
6.  George Orwell, *1984* (New York: New American Library, 1971), p.
    247.

purposes or for political or philosophical discussion." Furthermore, the grammar of Newspeak was simplified to the point where there was almost a complete interchangeability between different parts of speech. Any word could be used in either the verb, adjective, noun, or adverb form, usually without even altering the word itself.

The other major group of words fell into the B vocabulary, and this consisted of words specially constructed for political purposes. (The C vocabulary consisted purely of technical words and phrases of interest only to various specialists and technicians.) B words constituted a kind of "verbal shorthand," in all cases made up of compound words welded together in an easily pronounceable form. Acronyms and abbreviated contractions were particularly popular. Heretical words were either purged of their earlier meaning or dropped from the language altogether. Typical words in the B list included goodthink (orthodoxy), bellyfeel (blind enthusiastic acceptance), oldthink (wicked and decadent past ideas no longer acceptable), and finally, doublethink (the capacity to entertain simultaneously two contradictory notions without feeling the least bit uncomfortable). Euphemisms were very popular, e.g., "joy camps" referred to forced labor camps, and "Minipax" designated the ministry of peace which was in effect the ministry of war. To discourage all thought, especially of a critical kind, the vocabulary was constantly being shrunken. New words and abbreviations were replacing older more complex formulations. The entire Declaration of Independence of the United States of America, for example, could be reduced to a single word: *crimethink*. The language of Oceania provided the most effective means for controlling the political (or rather, nonpolitical) behavior of its inhabitants.

Similar concerns with the abuse of language in real contemporary society have been expressed by Herbert Marcuse. In particular he finds what he calls "the language of total administration" offensive and stupefying. All of the tendencies described by Orwell seem to have appeared, including the use of contracted forms and acronyms. During the Vietnam war we became so inured to the abuse of language, that we found nothing remarkable in reports of heavy fighting in the "demilitarized zone," we accepted without question the characterization of napalm attacks on innocent villagers as "pacification," and we even came to accept the description of the systematic stripping of the Vietnamese countryside with chemicals and napalm as "forced draft modernization." We also accepted terms for the enemy that effectively dehumanized him. In short we were well on the way to a rather sophisticated form of doublethink. Nor did the Watergate obscenity deliver us from this fate. Nixon's aides invented new terms and redefined the meaning of older ones to help obscure the nature of their acts. When they lied they said they had "misspoken" themselves. When previous lies were contradicted by overwhelming evidence, these previous statements became "inoperative." It is hard to tell whether "Nixonese" was consciously modeled on the principles of Newspeak, or whether the similarities are purely coincidental.

Herbert Marcuse argues that the situation has deteriorated to the point where we are badly in need of "linguistic therapy" to help re-establish the meaning of concepts totally distorted by the Establishment. He looks with favor on the use of swear words and other epithets by the New Left to characterize the Establishment. To call a policeman a pig is for Marcuse a kind of liberating act, perhaps capable of generating a "new sensibility which would be critical of the existing order." [7]

---

7.  For discussion of some of these points, see Ian Slater, "Orwell, Marcuse, and the Language of Politics." Paper delivered to the June 1974 meetings of the Canadian Political Science Association, Toronto. A more general discussion of the "political sociology of language, socialization, and legitimation" appears in Claus Mueller, *The Politics of Communication* (New York: Oxford University Press, 1973). The chapter on "Distorted Communication" reports some fascinating research on the abuse of language by the Nazi régime.

A REDEFINITION OF POLITICS

The analysis just completed suggests a redefinition of politics not simply in terms of authority but comprising as well, influence and power. Political science, therefore, involves the study of power, influence, *or* authority in whatever setting they might occur. Admittedly broad in sweep, this definition permits us to make sense of such otherwise baffling notions as the "politics of the family." It directs our attention to the formal vertical relationships which usually embody authority and to the less structured relationships of power and influence. By studying various forms of communication we are able to identify the nature of the relationships and perhaps go on to evaluate the "success rate" of various actors' different communication attempts. Who is able to use the language of authority successfully? When does a "power statement" work, and when is influence more effective? Answers to these questions permit us to estimate the "amount" of power, influence, or authority different actors "possess."

Small group experiments tend to show that authority (e.g., of teachers or lecturers) is less effective than influence (e.g., of fellow students or group discussion leaders) as an agent of attitude change. One difficulty in interpreting these experiments, however, stems from their concern with social structure rather than with the patterns of communication within structural settings. Thus, one experiment contrasted attitude change of individuals exposed only to lectures with individuals placed in a discussion group covering similar material. But these structural differences are only *prima facie* indicators of more fundamental differences in communications. Perhaps we may assume that lecturers usually consider themselves in authority roles and tend to use the language of authority whereas group discussion leaders are less authority-oriented and usually prefer influence language to authority. But this is not necessarily the case. A more interesting experiment would contrast

a)    an "authority" lecturer
b)    an "influence" lecturer
c)    an "authority" group discussion leader
d)    an "influence" group discussion leader

On the other hand, of course, certain roles and situations do lend themselves more to the use of one type of communication rather than another. We tend to use influence among *friends* or in a situation which is mutually defined as *cooperative*. (Nevertheless, the effectiveness of influence in small groups may depend on one's self-image vis-à-vis other group members. Generally, influence flows from high status "popular" individuals to low status "unpopular" individuals.)[8] We tend to use power among *enemies* or people with whom we feel ourselves in *competition*. *Authority* presupposes *vertical relationships* (e.g., parent to child, teacher to student, old to young, doctor to nurse, employer to employee, etc.)

These questions suggest yet another consequence of our analysis: the identification of certain *strategies* for political actors in terms of the predominant category of communication. The general problem of political strategy is best conceptualized in the vast literature that has grown up around the "theory of games." Fundamental to the game theory approach is the distinction between games of chance or skill on the one hand, and games of strategy on the other. The latter are characterized by the fact that "the best course of action for each player depends on what the other players do." In order to refine theoretical propositions describing (and prescribing) strategic behavior, researchers set up experimental situations (i.e., games) many of which explicitly attempt to illustrate the concept of *power*. But influence and authority tend to be overlooked. Experimenters often try to elimi-

---

8.    See, for example, J. C. Moore, Jr., "Status and Influence in Small Group Interactions," *Sociometry*, XXXI, 1, March 1968, pp. 47–63. The experiment mentioned above is reported in Elihu Katz and Paul F. Lazarsfeld, *Personal Influence* (New York: Free Press, 1955), pp. 74–81.

nate sources of influence (e.g., face-to-face encounters) when their subjects do not "behave properly" (i.e., as predicted). One experiment (using a kind of card game) set players against one another in a highly competitive, almost warlike situation in which winning meant wiping out all other players. To the experimenter's distress, individuals refused to "play to win" until he modified the experiment by building cardboard partitions which prevented players from seeing each other. I would interpret this modification as a fairly successful attempt to eliminate (nonverbal) influence communication in order to guarantee that the game would develop into a "pure power" conflict.

Despite his predominant interest in the elements of power games (those involving threats and promises), Thomas Schelling shows great sensitivity to influence considerations in issuing the following note of caution for game theorists: "There is no way to build a model for the interaction of two or more decision units . . . by purely formal deduction. An analyst can deduce the decisions of a single rational mind if he knows the criteria that govern the decisions; but he cannot infer by purely formal analysis what can pass between two centers of consciousness." [9]

In general, however, the game theory literature lacks a concept of influence which might sensitize experimenters to the significance of such actions on their part as "illustrating strategies," "going over the rules," and so on. I am suggesting that we learn more about behavior by treating the entire experimental setting as our laboratory. (Certainly this was the thrust of the Milgram studies reported in Chapter 2.) But most experiments masquerade as "power games" even though influence games and authority games are going on at the same time. The language the experimenter uses to describe various strategies will definitely *influence* the players' perception of that strategy (e.g., if agreeing to cooperate is called "yielding," players will probably avoid coopera-

9. Thomas Schelling, *The Strategy of Conflict* (New York: Oxford University Press, 1963), p. 163. The earlier quote defining games of strategy appears on p. 5.

tion for fear of "losing face." A similar point about the influence of terminology underlies S. I. Hayakawa's hypothetical contrast between two communities' responses to unemployment.[10] One community treats the unemployed as social failures and puts them on "welfare"; the other treats them as temporarily disadvantaged and set up a "social insurance scheme" against which "citizen policy-holders" advance "claims." The obvious conclusion confirms the proverb that "if you call a dog a dirty name he'll live up to it.")

Game theory experimenters likewise seem blind to the presence of authority in the experimental setting in the form of rules, instructions, and so on. While focusing attention on what the "subject" (notice the terminology) will do presumably in response to the strategic moves of *other players,* experimenters ignore their *own* influence and authority as important determinants of subjects' behavior. We should, in short, re-examine the experimental evidence to determine the role of authority (giving players "instructions" on how to play) and of influence (changing perceptions of the payoff structure and/or altering the values of players), as well as of power (use by players of threats and promises to change the "objective" payoffs of various moves). But we can go even further by designing new games in which players have a choice between power strategies *and* influence strategies. We could then observe their behavior to discover when influence will be attempted rather than power, what responses it evinces, and so forth.

The question of influence versus power strategies cuts across the distinction between "mixed motive" and "competitive" (or "zero-sum") games. In both types of games, players may use either a pure "power" strategy consisting of threats and promises (e.g., if you move there I'll move here); or an influence strategy (if you move there you'll feel cheated). Without using the above

10.  See S. I. Hayakawa, *Language in Action* (New York: Harcourt, Brace, 1941), pp. 3–14.

terminology, Thomas Schelling has nevertheless invented a hypothetical game designed precisely to identify the impact of mutual influence on a mixed motive power game. His hypothetical experiment would require use of a machine that would convey the players' value systems to each other by recording their affective reaction to various outcomes. Schelling speculates that this experiment would demonstrate that players' reactions "are subject to a mutual interaction that results from the fact that each knows that his own visible reaction is yielding information about his own expectations."

Schelling's machine adds influence communication to a relationship otherwise limited to power exchanges. He feels that such information is naturally present, though, in most human interactions, especially those that are face-to-face. We learn to "read" others' expressions, especially to judge how they are "decoding" what we say. This information in turn influences our strategies and responses. To paraphrase Hamlet, there is more to the real world of political games than is dreamt of in any game theoretic interpretation.

Nevertheless, when we shift attention from the experimental setting to the "real world," we can similarly distinguish political power strategies from influence strategies. A power strategy presupposes (apparent) control of some important resource or value which can be manipulated through threats and promises; however, an influence strategy can be adopted even by those poor in such resources. The skillful influence politician can often perform seeming miracles through suggestion, prediction, and advice that make possible a kind of political "jiujitsu," (a term used by Gene Sharp to characterize strategies of nonviolence). Although nonviolence can constitute a power strategy, important elements of it are based on influence. The nonviolent demonstrator, for example, puts himself at the mercy of the superior power of his opponent but attempts through tacit or explicit uses of influence to overcome this disadvantage. The demonstrator who lies down in front of someone's car mutely says, "I recognize that you have the power to run over me, *but if you do so you will be a murderer* and I a public monument to your cruelty and injustice." In this instance, the influencer attempts to set up an internal conflict of conscience in order to neutralize his opponent's superior power. But if his opponent lacks a conscience. . . . (One is reminded of Governor George Wallace's defiant declaration that any demonstrator who lay down in front of *his* car would do so for the last time.)

Such dramatic possibilities of failure notwithstanding, influence strategies deserve far greater attention from both experimenters (game theorists) and practitioners (political leaders).[11] One advantage of an influence strategy is that it may result in less hostility or resentment than a power strategy. Our culture tends to sensitize us more to the coercive nature of power than of influence. We are not unique in this regard. An ancient Chinese proverb makes exactly the same point:

> When people are subdued by force
> they do not submit in heart.
> They submit because their strength
> is not adequate to resist.
> But when they are subdued by virtue,
> they are pleased in their inner hearts,
> and they submit sincerely.
>
> (Mencius, Chinese philosopher c. 300 B.C.)

The politics of "black power" in the late sixties and early seventies in the United States probably engendered a far greater backlash than did the politics of black influence that preceded it. On the other hand, however, because black politics had widened its strategic horizons to encompass power, more maneuverability

11. It is probably not coincidental that this suggestion comes from a Canadian. As a nation relatively poor in resources for international *power* politics, Canada has tried to elaborate a concept of "quiet diplomacy" that places considerable faith in the efficacy of *influence*. Contrasts to the "carrot and stick" style of Canada's southern neighbor need not be labored. (To the extent that international politics is anarchic, the use of *authority* strategies is inappropriate.)

was afforded influence politicians who could add to their strategic repertoire a new credible prediction: if you do not pass reforms, the ghettos will explode again.

## POLITICAL TALK AND THE PRESIDENTIAL TAPES

Most people read the Presidential transcripts to decide for themselves the guilt or innocence of Richard Nixon. The transcripts are important for other purposes as well: to a student of "politics as talk," the transcripts provide an almost undreamed of opportunity to "listen in" on politics at the highest level of the United States government. There is, of course, a problem of validity that has troubled everyone who has had access to the transcripts. Cartoonist Doug Sneyd conveyed these misgivings brilliantly in the cartoon that shows an aide bringing President Nixon "some good news and some bad news: the Presidential transcripts are on the bestsellers' list, but in the fiction category." Similarly, questions were raised concerning the reliability of the transcripts. Two different typists' transcriptions of the same portion of tape appeared by accident in the published edition, and the differences between each version attracted widespread publicity. (See *Time,* May 27, 1974, p. 20.)

Problems of validity and reliability notwithstanding, we can explore on the basis of the transcripts important aspects of Richard Nixon's politics as revealed in what he and his advisers purportedly said to one another. Particularly intriguing are the conversations between John Dean (at the time the President's counsel) and Mr. Nixon. Even through the emotionless medium of cold print, we sense the deferential attitude of Dean to Nixon. "Good morning, sir." ". . . excuse me." "All right sir." "That will be done." (Feb. 28, 1973). In contrast to Dean's deferential posture, Nixon assumes the role of authority figure, even when he uses "influence language." He says to Dean, "So you see, I think you better have a good, hard, face-to-face talk with him and say . . ." (p. 44). Immediately afterward, Nixon solidifies this "suggestion" into an "order."

"You have a talk with him and say we had a talk about this. . . ." Nixon is clearly "in authority," but he looks to his advisers for information and suggestions. Sometimes he "draws them out" by "bouncing ideas off them." Their task is primarily one of prediction, of intelligent speculation regarding the outcome of alternative strategies or the creative input of suggesting new ones.

> "I think after the Gray thing takes one course or the other, there will be a dead period of news on Watergate until the Ervin hearings start again." [p. 69]

> "Well, then you will get a barrage of questions probably . . ." [p. 69]

> "He is going to lay it out, and just all hell is going to break loose once he does it. It is going to change the atmosphere of the Gray hearings and it is going to change the atmosphere of the whole Watergate hearings." [p. 71]

While each of these statements constitutes an influence statement, a prediction intended to offset the President's assessment of the situation and therefore his choice of actions and responses, the following statement is a classic of influence, paradigmatic in terms of our earlier categories.

> There is a certain domino situation here. If some things start going, a lot of other things are going to start going, and there can be alot of problems if everything starts falling. So there are dangers Mr. President, I would be less than candid if I didn't tell you there are. There is a reason for not everyone going up and testifying. [p. 87]

Sometimes the adviser merely supplies information in order to provide the authority figure a better basis for decision. Dean proposes that the President would benefit from "maybe about 30 minutes of just my recitation to you of fact so that you operate from the same facts that everyone else has." When Nixon agrees,

Dean further explains that he will, "Just paint the whole picture for you, the soft spots, the potential problem areas . . . and the like so that when you make judgments you will have all that information" (p. 94).

The overall impact of these remarkable documents is to provide almost for the first time a peek behind the curtain that hides "backstage politics." As raw data for the student of "politics as talk," the transcripts could not be more appropriate: the one word that constantly recurs in the transcripts is "talk" itself. Nixon and his advisers understand intuitively the central proposition of this approach to politics. They repeatedly "rehearse" entire conversations in hypothetical situations, for example, planning what John Dean might say in his "testimony" before the Ervin committee. They calculate with great precision the sequence of conversations necessary to "get" certain people to "do" or "say" certain things. Always the emphasis is on talk.

[Dean] ". . . John Connolly is close to Patman and if anyone could *talk turkey* to Patman, Connolly could. . . . Stan is going to see Jerry Ford and try to *brief* him and explain to him the problems he has." [p. 39]

[President] "Jerry should *talk* to Widnall. . . ." [p. 39]

[Dean] "I think Maury could *talk* to Ford. . . ." [p. 41]

[Haldeman] "I will *talk* to Cook." [p. 41]

[President] "Maybe Ehrlichman should *talk* to him. Ehrlichman understands the law." [p. 41]

[Emphasis added]

The ironic outcome of the Watergate melodrama, in which the "men of influence" went to jail while the "man of authority" received an unconditional, absolute pardon ought to alert all of us to a number of normative questions for which traditional philosophies of politics seem inappropriate. Politics involves neither authority relations nor power relations alone, but any social relationship in which either power, influence or authority is featured. As students of politics, we have been aware of the need to discuss an ethics of authority (notwithstanding Richard Nixon's irresponsible conduct), but we have been terribly remiss in considering the ethical questions related to the exercise of power and influence.[12] By the same token, the poverty of our conceptualizations of these phenomena has contributed to a deleterious lag of theory behind practice, and in some cases has even interfered with sophisticated understanding of practice itself. Faced with the dilemma of how to act, an actor who conceptualizes the world in purely power terms necessarily will be incapable of using influence. Yet surely this form of relationship has, in the past thirty years, undergone a profound transformation understood in a practical manner by admen and women's liberationists, but almost totally ignored by political scientists.

12.    An important exception to this generalization is John O'Neill, who draws on the work of Paulo Freire, Frantz Fanon, and Jerry Rubin (among others) to articulate an ethics of political language use. See John O'Neill, "Violence, Language and the Body Politic," in *Sociology as a Skin Trade* (New York: Harper and Row, 1972); and "Le Langage et la décolonisation," *Sociologie et Société* VI, 2, Nov. 1974; and *Making Sense Together: An Introduction to Wild Sociology* (New York: Harper and Row, 1974).

# Appendix A:
# The Poverty of
# Political Science Concepts

One by-product of the "behavioral movement" in political science was a fascination with numbers almost at the expense of words. Many behavioralists, intent on adapting what they conceived to be the techniques of "science" to the study of politics, insisted on approaches employing "hard" data which could be manipulated using "statistical" and other "quantitative" methods of analysis. Underlying their faith in such approaches was the conviction that numbers brought them closer to "the truth"; that quantitative precision and technical sophistication added an entirely new dimension of insight; and that as scientists we had better get on with our first task: measurement and "data gathering." The collection of "hard data" would be followed in later stages by "data analysis"—aggregation of data through such operations as factor analysis, tests for "statistical significance," etc. Even the sophisticated "second generation" of quantitative political scientists who emerged in the mid-sixties focused attention on fleshing out this research paradigm in terms of a more cautious use of operations such as "causal-modeling" (which rested on seemingly doubtful assumptions about the "real world,") and so on. The concern was, in short, how to use numbers more intelligently. A vast literature and controversy grew up around the question of the distribution of power in America, but most of the disagreement focused on how to measure power rather than how to conceptualize it. Not until the early 1970's did someone of stature and prestige make the fatally obvious point that "Before you can measure, you must know first what it is that you are measuring." At approximately the same time, Karl Deutsch announced in his presidential address to the American Political Science Association that certain "traditional" approaches to the study of politics were not simply "out-of-date and soon to be discarded for the new beauties of computer tape," because "we cannot test or measure anything that we have not recognized first." [1]

In some respects, however, this advice came too late. The reduction of political science to quantitative technique ensured that a number of the bright young graduate students trained in largely "behavioral" departments grew up in a poverty-stricken conceptual environment. Taught that concepts are merely statements of certain "operational" (and therefore commensurable) attributes, purely empirical in nature, these political scientists suffered an "occupational incapacity" to deal adequately with the formation and analysis of concepts. For them power is best defined in terms of the easiest way to measure (something). Several scholars, entranced by this circular argument, counseled disparagingly that since we seemed unable to derive satisfactory measures we should *abolish* the term altogether! Giovanni Sartori speaks directly to this point declaring that:

> In this messy confrontation about quantification and its bearing on standard logical rules we simply tend to forget that *concept formation stands prior to quantification.* The process

1.  Giovanni Sartori, "Concept Misformation in Comparative Politics," *American Political Science Review,* vol. 64, December 1970, p. 1038. Karl W. Deutsch "Political Theory and Political Action," *ibid,* vol. 65, March 1971, p. 22.

of thinking inevitably begins with a qualitative (natural) language, no matter at which shore we shall subsequently land.[2]

Not all efforts to define power commit the circular fallacy of "operationalism" (i.e., attempting to derive some type of empirical measure which is then taken to stand for the phenomenon itself). A far more prevalent conceptual error is to collapse or obscure important differences among social interactions, classifying them all jointly under a single heading (usually "power").

For example, J. David Singer has written that his "purpose is to seek a clarification of the concept of power by the presentation of a formal, analytic model of . . . influence." Singer also notes in a footnote that Robert Dahl "tends to use 'power' and 'influence' interchangeably." Christian Bay announces that " 'Power' and 'influence' are in this book synonymous terms. I believe this is the most confusion-proof way of relating the two terms to one another, given the wide overlap in their usage, in scientific journals as well as in everyday language." Similarly, Herbert Simon insisted that "It is not necessary . . . to distinguish between influence and power, and I shall continue to use the two words as synonyms." As editor of an important collection of "studies in social power," Dorwin Cartwright observes that "throughout [the book], power is viewed as the ability of one person (or group) to influence or control some aspect of another person (or group)." Finally, John Harsanyi states simply that "power . . . essentially is an ability to exert influence." [3]

Thus writers like Dahl, Singer, Simon, and others slip back

2. Sartori, "Concept Misformation," p. 1038.
3. J. David Singer, "Inter-Nation Influence: A Formal Model," *American Political Science Review,* vol. 57, 1963, p. 420 and footnote 3; Christian Bay, *The Structure of Freedom* (Stanford: Stanford University Press, 1958), p. 248n.; Herbert Simon, "Notes on the Observation and Measurement of Political Power," *Journal of Politics,* November 1953, footnote 2; Dorwin Cartwright, "Preface" to *Studies in Social Power* (Ann Arbor: University of Michigan Press, 1959), p. v; John Harsanyi, in Martin Shubik, ed., *Game Theory and Related Approaches to Social Behavior* (New York: John Wiley & Sons, 1964).

and forth from one term to another, effectively precluding a priori the analysis of distinctions however illuminating such an analysis might prove. Ironically, the distinction we have drawn between a power relation and an influence relation is aptly (though unintentionally) illustrated by Robert Dahl:

> Suppose the chances are about one out of a hundred that one of my students, Jones, will read *The Great Transformation* during the holidays—even if I do not mention the book to him. Suppose that if I mention the book to him and ask him to read it, the chances are still only one out of a hundred. Then it accords with my intuitive notions of power to say that evidently I have no power over Jones with respect to his reading *The Great Transformation* during the holidays—at least not if I restrict the basis of my action to mentioning the book and asking him (politely) to read it. Guessing this to be the case, I tell Jones that if he does not read the book over the holidays I shall fail him in my course. Suppose now that the chances he will read the book are about 99 out of 100. . . .[4]

Following our classification, Dahl's polite suggestion that Jones read the book constituted an attempt to "influence" Jones; while Dahl's explicit threat to invoke a sanction constituted, of course, a power relation.

Besides providing a striking example of the difference between influence and power, the above illustration demonstrates convincingly that Robert Dahl has no place in his conceptual repertoire for what we here define as influence. Whenever he differentiates the terms (and he seldom does) it is on the basis of the *severity* (rather than the presence or absence) of sanctions. In this usage Dahl follows a convention established by Lasswell and Kaplan who defined power as "a form of influence [!] in which the effect on policy is enforced or expected to be enforced by *relatively severe* sanctions." [5]

4.  Robert Dahl, "The Concept of Power," *Behavioral Science* II, July 1957.
5.  Lasswell and Kaplan, *Power and Society*.

Despite (explicit) pretensions to the contrary, the argument in Lasswell and Kaplan is surprisingly confused and inconsistent. In the book we are told first that power is a "form of influence," then in another place that "It is the threat of sanctions which differentiates power from influence in general"; and finally that the severity of sanctions is the touchstone. Much of the confusion is exemplified in the following statement: "The *base value* of an influence relation is that which is the condition for the exercise of the influence in question. The *power base* is the value which is the condition for participation in decision making in the given case." [6]

Ironically, to the extent that it has been persuasive, the image of man which has fostered the belief that "only power counts" itself manifests the phenomenon of "influence." Those who cling to this belief have thereby precluded an explanation of what influenced them to take such a posture. Few would argue that they had been either forced (threatened) or *bribed* (promised) to do so.

6.   *Ibid.,* p. 84. (Emphasis added.)

# Appendix B:
# A Critique of B.F. Skinner

The analysis of power and influence in Chapter 1 has several direct implications for the "behavioral" theories of B. F. Skinner and like-minded psychologists.[1] Behaviorists contend that sanctions (or in Skinner's terminology, "reinforcing consequences") absolutely determine human behavior, and conversely, that all human behavior can and must be "explained" by analysis of the contingencies of reinforcement that "generated" it. Moreover, such an explanation can be formulated "without appealing to hypothetical inner states or processes" (COR, p. 8). As we have done with sanctions, Skinner differentiates "positive" from "negative" reinforcers on the basis of "whether they reinforce when they appear [positive] or disappear [negative]" (COR, p. 7). Apparently, therefore, our concept of power is entirely compatible

1. This critique examines the following works of B. F. Skinner, *Science and Human Behavior* (New York: Macmillan Co., 1953); *Verbal Behavior* (New York: Appleton-Century-Crofts, 1957); *Contingencies of Reinforcement: A Theoretical Analysis* (New York: Appleton-Century-Crofts, 1969); *Beyond Freedom and Dignity* (New York: Alfred A. Knopf, 1971). For convenience the books are cited in text by the abbreviations SHB, VB, COR, and BFD respectively.

with Skinner's theoretical framework. But our concept of influence would appear to him nonsensical. To manipulate behavior, one must manipulate the environment in such a way that the desired behavior is somehow reinforced, positively or negatively. But influence as we have defined it does not manipulate contingencies of reinforcement, as power purports to do. Still, we have maintained that influence can effectively change behavior.

Why is Skinner apparently unable to formulate an influence concept? I think the answer has to do with the origins of his model in experiments with rats and pigeons. On the assumption that man is "not essentially different from the lower animals . . . every human characteristic, including consciousness and reasoning power, could be found in other species" (COR, p. 223), Skinner has felt little compunction about basing most of his propositions about human behavior on experimental situations. Skinner seems always to think in terms of this paradigm; he often illustrates his concepts and theories by explicit reference to experiments in which positive or negative reinforcements "condition" certain patterns of behavior in pigeons or rats.[2] He then reasons from these situations to analogues in the human world.

Since, however, barely any elements of a language exist between pigeon or rat and experimenter, it is no wonder that the phenomenon of influence (which we have already established takes the form of advice, warning, etc.) disappears from sight. How can one speak of "advising" a rat? In our terminology, while experimenters have considerable power over the animals they use, they have virtually no influence with them.

The situation is rather amusing. Skinner and his associates work for weeks using a power process (conditioning) to "train" rats and pigeons to "behave." They then transpose their hypothesis (presumably now validated) to the human sphere and elaborate

2. For example, in a list of eighteen terms related to contingencies of reinforcement, thirteen are defined explicitly with reference to experimental settings using rats or pigeons. Presumably these terms are immediately transferable to human situations. (See COR, pp. 22–25.)

a fairly sophisticated "theory" of human behavior, the central assumption of which is, "only power counts." Had they *started* with humans, influence might have accomplished the desired "training" in a few brief seconds: Skinner need only have advised his subjects, "If you push the button, you will receive food (etc.)."

There are, however, some problems with this illustration because the "reward" (food) is presumably distributed by the experimenter. Thus despite the superficial appearance of the communication, what the experimenter is really saying is, "If you push this button, I will give you food" (power). The difficulty vanishes, however, if we postulate the intervention of a "third party" who simply advises the "subject" that the "experimenter" will reward or punish certain types of behavior. Although the dyadic relationship (i.e., between experimenter and subject) characteristic of most behavioral experiments precludes such an arrangement, the "real world" of course does not.[3] The following illustration shows the importance of expanding the network of relationships beyond a dyad.

THE RAT REVISITED: RITUAL AND
RELIGION AS INFLUENCE

In a note to Chapter 1 of *Contingencies of Reinforcement,* Skinner provides a list of terms that specify certain interrelations among stimuli and responses in an "experimental space" (i.e., laboratory) used to study the behavior of animals. Included in this

3.  It should be noted that Skinner touches briefly on the possibility of using "instructions" in place of reinforcements, but the discussion fails to take account of the distinction between instructions as power and instructions as influence (or, for that matter, as authority). Having essentially blinded himself to the possibility of gaining insight through such an analysis, Skinner effectively dismisses the subject with the simple (undefended) assertion that "verbal communication is not . . . a substitute for the arrangement and manipulation of ["independent"] variables." (COR, p. 115).

    We shall return to this aspect of Skinner's myopia later on when we discuss the distinction between "brute facts" and "institutional facts."

space are "various sources of stimuli such as sounds and light, and reinforcing devices such as a food or water dispenser. . . ." The terms in the list are "defined" by reference to the nature of the stimuli and the type of behavior they produce, e.g., escape, avoidance, stimulus discrimination, etc.

Curiously, the sixth term in this list is "superstition" (Skinner's quotation marks). In this situation, Skinner informs us, reinforcement is programmed to occur at fixed intervals regardless of the behavior of the rat. In effect, therefore, any behavior that occurs "just before the appearance of the food is reinforced, and similar coincidences become more likely as the behavior is strengthened." Thus the rat tends to engage in behavior that "leads to" reinforcement. But because the program of reinforcement is in fact independent of the behavior of the rat, the connection between its behavior and reinforcement is spurious. Skinner bluntly states, "The rat develops a 'superstitious ritual.' " [4]

The analogy between the rat's superstitious ritual and human religious practices seems clear enough. Skinner appears to have cast new light on a very interesting problem, namely, the phenomenon of ritual behavior in human societies. Such rituals are really conceived as ways of producing certain reinforcing consequences although "in reality" the consequences are unrelated to the ritual. (Think of a tribal rain dance.)

Without gainsaying Skinner's interesting suggestion that rituals may be learned through a conditioning process in which "spuriously related" reinforcements are forthcoming on at least some occasions consequent to the performance of the ritual, I would like to show another facet of influence entirely beyond the ken of

---

4. Though Skinner would abhor such an analysis, I would contend that this experiment documents the importance of perception and construction of the situation even in rat behavior. Superstition may be manifested as ritual behavior, but it surely rests on an "internal mental state," namely, the (mis)perception on the part of the rat that its behavior "causes" the reward to appear. Moreover, manipulation of such misperception is precisely the basis for the type of influence discussed below.

his analysis. For rituals in human society, in contrast to the "private" ritual of the lone rat in a laboratory experiment, are often collectively institutionalized. To duplicate the human situation we would have to expand the dyad of experimenter-rat to at least a tryad by positing the intervention of an "adviser to the rat." Assuming the adviser could speak rat language, he might then interpret the ritual to the rat in terms of some kind of theory or doctrine about a *deus ex machina* (the experimenter) who rewards the ritualistic behavior. In short, the adviser could invent a "religion" for which he would presumably be qualified to serve as "high priest."

That Skinner is insensitive to the possible relationship between high priest and true believer follows from his obsession with the rat in the box as a paradigm for all behavior; though rats may develop what humans call superstitious rituals, it is inconceivable that they could develop the institution of religion. "Power will do" to analyze rat behavior; one badly needs a concept of influence to understand humans. Since perceptions are "under the skin," in Skinner's terms, they lie outside of the range of valid facts for scientific inquiry. Thus it is not surprising that he is incapable of formulating a concept of influence.[5] But explaining Skinner's myopia, and excusing it, are entirely different matters.

5.  Noam Chomsky makes a related criticism at several points in his review of *Beyond Freedom and Dignity*. For example, he asserts that "Skinner has no way of dealing with the factors involved in persuading someone or changing his mind." But Chomsky himself devotes little sustained analysis to these factors beyond such bald statements as his claim that "for an argument to be persuasive, at least to a rational person, it must be coherent. . . ."

    Ironically, in what he takes to be a "counter-example" to Skinner's theory of behavior modification, Chomsky unwittingly illustrates influence of the "second-person hypothetical" type (see Ch. I above). "Suppose that your doctor gives you a very persuasive argument to the effect that *if you continue to smoke, you will die a horrible death* from lung cancer. . . ." [Emphasis added]

    Instead of pursuing the importance of this statement as an example of the use of influence to change perception (rather than power

REINFORCERS: WHAT KIND OF FACTS?

If Skinner's laboratory-based methodology has affected his image of man, so has his theory of knowledge. Repeatedly he reminds us that his approach places the study of behavior on a solid "scientific" foundation, relying on "techniques of direct observation" rather than the nebulous "hypothetico-deductive methods" used by "mentalistic philosophers" who refer to "inaccessible events— some of them fictitious, others irrelevant." By contrast behaviorists examine "conspicuous" facts that can easily be observed and interpreted without reference to "mentalistic" propositions about "hypothetical inner states" of the organism. The beauty of contingency analysis, Skinner assures us, is that the scientist can see what he is talking about. He confines himself to the realm of "hard facts," focusing on what he can see and, more importantly, often manipulate. The world for Skinner is divided into "independent variables" (environmental contingencies) and "dependent variables" (behavioral responses). This "empirical epistemology" leads to a radical rejection of introspection as a technique for gaining knowledge:

> Instead of concluding that man can know only his subjective experiences—that he is bound forever to his private world and that the external world is only a construct—a behavioral theory of knowledge suggests that it is the private world which, if not entirely unknowable, is at least not likely to be known well. [COR, p. 228]

Skinner grudgingly admits a possible relevance for "mentalistic theories designed to bridge the gap between dependent and

---

to change contingency), Chomsky dilutes his criticism by asking, "Is it necessarily the case that this argument will be less effective in modifying your behavior than any arrangement of true reinforcers?" In other words, Chomsky fails to drive home the point that Skinner's theory is defective because it lacks a concept of influence. (See Chomsky, *New York Review of Books,* December 30, 1971, p. 21.)

independent variables in the analysis of behavior" (COR, p. 240), but hastily adds that "we should certainly welcome *other* ways of treating the data more satisfactorily" (COR, p. 241). Indeed, he points out, attempts to formulate mentalistic theories fall back on one or other versions of the "Inner Man." This curious little fellow (also called "homunculus") is pictured as "doing" things under the skin or inside the head to activate our feelings, perceptions, and ultimately our actions. Sardonically, Skinner derides Freud's notions of the superego, ego and id: "multiple Inner Men who struggle with each other, the outcome determining the behavior of the body they inhabit."

To attain "scientific precision," such murky, mysterious pseudo-data must be purged. Despite the popular attractiveness of explanations that attempt to tell the "Inside Story," we must "dispossess the Inner Man by replacing him with genetic and environmental variables" (COR, p. 273). Only on the firm foundation of hard, conspicuous facts can the edifice of behavioral science be erected.

But there are facts and facts. Skinner seems to believe that science must concern itself only with what the philosopher John Searle calls "brute facts." The concept of brute facts is "easy to recognize but hard to describe": Searle relates it to a certain "picture of the world" which, for want of a more appropriate term, he labels "classical." According to the classical picture, the world consists of brute facts and therefore knowledge of the world takes a particular form: "[T]he concepts which make up the knowledge are essentially physical, or in [the] . . . dualistic version, either physical or mental." Furthermore, "the model for systematic knowledge of this kind is generally supposed to be simple empirical observations recording sense experiences." [6]

Although the use of "classical" concepts makes a great deal of sense when we are referring to the physical world in which brute facts are an apparent reality, the classical picture of the world is

6. Searle, *Speech Acts*, p. 50.

totally inappropriate for describing certain relationships in the social or human world. In short, the language of brute facts is not exhaustive of the totality of facts about the world. Again in Searle's words, "There are many kinds of facts and facts which obviously are objective facts and not matters of opinion or sentiment or emotion at all, which are hard, if not impossible, to assimilate to [the classical picture of the world]." Searle gives the following examples: "Mr. Smith married Miss Jones; the Dodgers beat the Giants 3–2 in 11 innings; Green was convicted of larceny; and Congress passed the Appropriations Bill." It is simply not possible, he contends, to describe facts like these in terms of the physical or even mental concepts appropriate to the classical picture. Although there are certain physical movements, states, and "raw feels" involved in such events as marriage ceremonies, baseball games, trials, and legislative actions, a description of these events in those terms alone would be quite inadequate. For example, Searle continues, let us assume that a group of highly trained observers are attempting to describe an American football game in statements only of brute facts:

> What could they say by way of description? Well within certain areas a good deal could be said, and using statistical techniques certain "laws" could even be formulated. For example, we can imagine that after a time our observer would discover the law of periodical clustering: at statistically regular intervals, organisms in light coloured shirts cluster together in roughly circular fashion (the huddle). Furthermore at equally regular intervals, circular clustering is followed by linear clustering (the teams line-up for the play), and linear clustering is followed by the phenomenon of linear interpenetration. Such laws would be statistical in character, and none the worse for that. But no matter how much data of this sort we imagine our observers to collect and no matter how many inductive generalizations we imagine them to make from the data, they still have not described American football. What is missing from their description? What is missing are all those concepts which are backed by *constitutive rules,* concepts such as touchdown, off side, game, points, first down, time out, etc., and

consequently what is missing are all the true statements one can make about a football game using those concepts.[7]

In other words, the world of human interaction takes place in the context of certain institutions which are underlaid by a system of rules in the form "X counts as Y in context C." It is to relationships of this kind that Searle attaches the name "institutional facts" to distinguish them from the "brute facts" of the classical picture. Language and linguistic behavior are to be understood in this context as the use of words in accordance with the "constitutive rules" embodied in grammar and syntax.

That the entire picture of the world implied by the notion of "institutional facts" lies outside Skinner's analytical framework is evident from some remarks found in the beginning of *Beyond Freedom and Dignity* which praise the methods of physics and biology as a model for the study of human behavior. Skinner correctly asserts that modern natural science had to free itself from the teleological conceptions inherent in Greek physics and biology. Aware that their own actions appeared to be governed by considerations of purpose and value (or *telos*), the Greeks imputed similar attributes to the natural world as well. Thus the account of an event like a stone rolling down the hill would be formulated with reference to the attempt by the stone to achieve the goal of reaching the bottom of the hill. Admittedly this framework is inappropriate for the study of natural events, which modern science views as mechanistically rather than teleologically determined. But for the modern social scientists to borrow for social explanation the mechanistic image of causation which natural science found useful for explanations of physical events is to commit the Greek error in reverse. Just as it is inappropriate to inquire what reasons a stone has for rolling down the hill, so it is similarly inappropriate to ask what caused a man to walk across the street, unless we wish to reduce the actions of the man to a

7. *Ibid.,* p. 52. (Emphasis added.)

set of mere physical movements. A similar point is made by the philosopher J. L. Austin:

> The sense in which saying something produces effects on other persons, or *causes* things is a fundamentally different sense of cause from that used in physical causation by pressure, etc. It has to operate through the conventions of language and is a matter of influence exerted by one person on another: this is probably the original sense of cause.[8]

It should be apparent by now that the range of phenomena referred to by the concepts power, influence, and authority are institutional facts rather than brute facts. Admittedly there are brute facts contained within these institutional facts. A power situation in which an armed robber holds up a bank involves a number of prominent brute facts: the gun, the bullets, the action of pulling the trigger, and so on. But the interpretation of the situation on the part of those involved in it constitutes a set of institutional facts, depending on mutual understanding of the language of threat, perception that guns are lethal weapons, and that bullets can punish someone severely. In short, a gun may be a brute fact, but its use in a power situation is an institutional fact. In a power situation, for example, the "constitutive rule" underlying the action is simply "In context C, action Y (verbal or otherwise) counts as a threat." Unless this rule is understood by both (all) participants, power can scarcely be said to exist. For power implies communication, and communication is an institutional fact.

To illustrate the importance of communication as a basis for power, one need only examine some extreme instances in which control of the "brute facts" of power is rendered useless because the institutional facts of communication and language are absent.

8. Austin, *How To Do Things with Words,* p. 112n. See also Floyd Matson, *The Broken Image* (New York: George Braziller, 1964); and Charles Taylor, *The Explanation of Behavior* (New York: Humanities Press, 1964).

Take the relationship between an infant and its parents. Undoubtedly the parents have a virtual monopoly of "power" in terms of such brute facts as control over the food intake, physical care, and exposure to "punishment" of the infant. But because the infant is incapable of understanding the contingencies which the parents might wish to link with these brute facts, the "power" of the parent to "force" or "bribe" the infant to behave is severely limited. "Threatening" an infant is a futile gesture, an extension of the language of power to a sphere in which its institutional bases are nonexistent. If violence evidences the failure of verbal power (i.e., the failure of a threat to be "effective"), then infant-beating poignantly illustrates the contrast between power as institutional fact and violence (literally) as brute fact.

Arthur Stinchcombe's discussion of the "man in a box" provides a second illustration. In this hypothetical example, a man is placed in a box "on the wall of which is a button he can push to electrocute a man outside the box." (This situation resembles an inverted Skinnerian experimental setup—its enactment as a melodrama might appropriately be entitled, "The Rat's Revenge.") Let us suppose, Stinchcombe continues, that the man in the box has no way of communicating with the man outside the box, except by pushing the electrocution button. It quickly becomes evident that while the man in the box holds the "power" of life and death over his potential victim, he enjoys little else. In order to convert this brute-fact (apparent) power into a useful device for controlling the victim's behavior, the man in the box must open up some form of communication with the man outside. A very rudimentary communication channel might consist of a set of signal lights outside the box instructing the victim to stand up or sit down. Provided that this device were accompanied by a "feedback" channel informing the man in the box that his "subject" [9] had complied, we could then assume that the man in the box had power over one aspect of the subject's behavior. Generalizing from

9.  The term suggests an ironic double entendre: both monarchs and experimenters have subjects.

this observation, Stinchcombe asserts, "As communication channels from inside to outside increase in capacity to discriminate among orders, and as those from outside to inside carry more information about the outside, power increases." [10] But despite the basis in brute facts of such a communication system (e.g., the electrical circuiting required for a signal light system) the important quality of the system would be its basis in institutional facts like shared meaning and mutual comprehension. The most sophisticated communication channels will not expand the power of the man in the box by one iota if his victim does not understand the signals that are intended to tell him what he is supposed to do. Nor, given the finality of the reinforcer to which he is exposed, will he have any opportunity to "learn" the proper responses through Skinnerian trial and error.

All of this accentuates the contrast between lower animal behavior and human behavior: our "learning" what a threat "means" differs from the pigeon's "learning" how to get rewards or avoid punishment. The pigeon "learns" the contingency "food" as a "brute fact." We learn the concept "threat" as an "institutional fact." [11] Humans, therefore, are able to generalize from the concept "threat," and the set of rules that define what counts as a threat, to deal with new cases in a way that the pigeon never could.[12]

10. Arthur Stinchcombe, *Constructing Social Theories* (New York: Harcourt, Brace & World, 1968), pp. 164–65.
11. Similarly criticizing the extension of laboratory vocabulary to human action, Chomsky demolishes Skinner's reinforcement theory of language with respect to the use of threats: "If the speaker has had a history of appropriate reinforcement . . . then he will tend to give the proper response when the threat which had previously been followed by the injury is presented. It would appear to follow from this description that a speaker will not respond properly to the mand *Your money or your life* unless he has a past history of being killed."
12. Cf. Searle, *Speech Acts,* p. 42: "Two of the marks of rule governed as opposed to merely regular behaviour [such as that which a pigeon might learn] are that we generally recognize deviations from the pattern as somehow wrong or defective and that the rule unlike the past regularity automatically covers new cases."

By now our portrait of Skinner has developed into a carica-
ture, drawn to accentuate certain difficulties inherent in his premises were they driven to their logical conclusion. But Skinner is
far too clever to do that. Especially in *Beyond Freedom and Dignity,* he qualifies and redirects the logic of his premises. At various points in the book, he devotes considerable attention to
"verbal stimuli." [13] But he has much difficulty explaining why some
verbal stimuli, especially those which we have here been calling
persuasion or influence are more effective than others. This is not
to say that he never mentions the term influence. In fact he presents at one point a fairly sophisticated discussion of it which is

Note, however, that Skinner raises a similar point in *Science and
Human Behavior* (p. 338) in the course of a discussion of "Government and the Law" as "Controlling Agencies." After stating that
commands function to bring "a selected repertoire of responses . . .
under the control of appropriate verbal stimuli," Skinner observes that,
"By establishing obedient behavior, the controlling agency prepares
for future occasions which it cannot otherwise foresee and for which
an explicit repertoire cannot, therefore, be prepared in advance. When
novel occasions arise to which the individual possesses no response,
he simply does as he is told."

The implications of "learning obedience" and the other potential
motivating factors which play a part in obedient behavior are discussed in Chapter 2 above.

13. Appropriately, Skinner's study of "Verbal Behavior" deals extensively
with the problem of classifying, analyzing, and explaining the effectiveness of verbal stimuli. Throughout the book Skinner sticks closely
to his behavioral epistemology, avoiding any temptation to introduce
concepts such as perception into his explanatory framework. Though
he does not elaborate the concepts of power, influence, or authority,
his whole enterprise concerns an analysis of how members of a
"verbal community" "control" and are controlled by verbal stimuli.
He coins several neologisms to help classify these stimuli, such as
the term "mand," which is derived from "command," "demand," etc.:
"[Mand] may be defined as a verbal operant in which the response is
reinforced by a characteristic consequence and is therefore under the
functional control of relevant conditions of deprivation or aversive
stimulation." (VB, pp. 35–36.) Note that this definition does not permit a distinction between "power" and "authority" nor does it distinguish between aversive stimulation as "action" and as "outcome"
(see below).

worth reproducing at length. Interestingly enough, this particular discussion of what we would term influence, occurs as part of a general discussion of the nature of value judgments or moral judgments in Skinner's theory of the behavioral process. He is attempting to show different ways in which we use the terms "should" and "ought" to "clarify nonsocial contingencies."

> To get to Boston you should (you ought to) follow route one is simply a way of saying "if you will be reinforced by reaching Boston, you will be reinforced if you follow route 1." [Note that this is an example of a second-person contingent statement.] To say that following route 1 is the "right" way to get to Boston is not an ethical or moral judgment but a statement about a highway system. Something closer to a value judgment may seem to be present in such an expression as "you should (you ought to) read David Copperfield" which may be translated, "you will be reinforced if you read *David Copperfield.*" It is a value judgment to the extent that it implies that the book will be reinforcing. We can bring the implication into the open by mentioning some of our evidence: "if you enjoyed *Great Expectations,* you should (you ought to) read David Copperfield." This value judgment is correct if it is generally true that those who are reinforced by *Great Expectations* are also reinforced by *David Copperfield.* [BFD, p. 179]

While Skinner is here concerned with the sense in which such a "value judgment" may be declared to be "correct," the statement to us exemplifies second-person contingent influence. For our purposes, the important consideration is not whether the statement is correct but whether it is believed, and furthermore whether it results in the behavior of reading *David Copperfield.* The example, however, does illustrate that Skinner tends not to distinguish conceptually between manipulating contingencies and providing information about contingencies. He may be correct in asserting that information about contingencies will only be important if it is supported by contingent outcomes. In fact I would agree with him on that point. But surely it makes a great deal of difference both to the resources necessary to affect behavior, and to the reaction expressed by the "subject," whether we are in fact manipulating contingencies or only providing information in the form of advice, warning, etc. Skinner glosses over this distinction to focus instead on the difference between positive and negative reinforcers.

In the final chapter of *Beyond Freedom and Dignity,* Skinner again returns to the role of verbal stimuli that take the form we have termed influence,[14] but he fails to develop the implications of his remarks.

> As listeners we acquire a kind of knowledge from the verbal behavior of others which may be extremely valuable in permitting us to avoid direct exposure to contingencies. We learn from the experience of others by responding to what they say about contingencies. When we are warned against doing something or are advised to do something, there may be no point in speaking of knowledge, but when we learn more durable kinds of warnings and advice in the form of maxims or rules, we may be said to have a special kind of knowledge about the contingencies to which they apply. [BFD, p. 179]

A further difficulty besets Skinner's peculiar attachment to a set of rather awkward concepts. Skinner claims to have invented a style of language which is "scientific" in the sense that he claims his whole theory is scientific. That is, it confines itself to the "observable facts," excluding reference to such inobservables as mentalistic activities, purposes, intentions, and so on. He sometimes speaks of restating prescientific description into this new language. Nevertheless, the linguistic framework he has adopted imposes upon Skinner some rather awkward problems. How do you describe "an accident" in terms of his scientific newspeak?

14. Earlier (BFD, p. 172) Skinner sarcastically rejects the term influence as a "softer" word which connotes "weak" forms of control: "If we are content merely to 'influence' people, we shall not get far from the original meaning of that word—'an ethereal fluid thought to flow from the stars and to affect the actions of men.' "

The important considerations, he has continually reminded us, are the contingencies of reinforcement. But in the usual sense of the term, a contingency is an artificial (i.e., man-created) situation. We literally make an outcome contingent upon the performance of a certain action. But a chance encounter with an aspect of the nonhuman environment is obviously not artificial. It would seem, therefore, not to "fit" the notion of contingency. But Skinner insists on carrying over the grammar of contingency analysis to precisely that type of encounter. His solution, therefore, to the problem of describing an accident is to personalize accidental encounters with the environment, introducing the concept of "natural" contingencies. Thus he refers at one point (BFD, p. 56) to "natural punishment" by which he means to describe the challenges that a difficult environment can pose for man. A few pages later (p. 59), he similarly characterizes the action of running head on into a wall in the almost absurd statement that "nature simply punishes [a man] when he runs into a wall." The same personalization is later applied to things in the statement (p. 85) that "things do not easily take control." Again (p. 98) there is his tautological assertion that "things that feel good *reinforce us* when we feel them." Perhaps the archetype for all of these statements can be found earlier in the book when he refers to the contingencies in an experiment which have been "arranged by the equipment," a statement remarkable for the erasure of human agency (and presumably, therefore, responsibility) that lies behind the design of a laboratory experiment. Indeed, the manner in which Skinner broadens the concept of contingency to cover all "aversive consequences" obscures the crucial distinction between "action" and "outcome." This strategy undoubtedly tends to support his claim that the concept of dignity (and its sister concept of responsibility) is irrelevant. But it becomes irrelevant through the impoverishing vocabulary that emerges from his laboratory-based image of the world.